TABLE OF CONTENTS

SECRETS OF MIND POWER

By
Harry Lorayne

Pustak Mahal®

DELHI • MUMBAI • BANGALORE • PATNA • HYDERABAD

Publishers :
Pustak Mahal, Delhi-110 006

Sales Centres:
• 6686, Khari Baoli, Delhi-110006 • *Ph.*: 2944314, 3911979
• 10-B, Netaji Subhash Marg, New Delhi-110002, *Ph.*: 3268292-93 *Fax*: 011-3280567

Administrative Office:
F-2/16 Ansari Road, Daryaganj, New Delhi-110002, *Ph.*: 3276539, 3272783, 3272784
• *Fax* : 011-3260518
E-mail: pustakmahal@vsnl.com

Branch Offices:
22/2 Mission Road (Shama Rao's Compound), Bangalore-560027
• *Ph.*: 2234025 *Fax*: 080-2240209
23-25 Zaoba Wadi, Thakurdwar (Opp. VIP Showroom), Mumbai-400002
• *Ph.*: 2010941 *Fax*: 022-2053387
Khemka House, Ist Floor, Opp. Women's Hospital, Ashok Rajpath, Patna-800004
• *Ph.*: 673644
5 - 1 - 707/1, Brij Bhavan, Bank Street, Kothi, Hyderabad- 500001
• *Ph.*: 4737530 *Fax*: 4737290

Published in India by arrangement with
LIFETIME BOOKS, INC.
Hollywood Blvd.,
Hollywood,

I.S.B.N. 81-223-0060-X

Edition : 2000

Printed at : Kwality Offset Printing Press, Naraina, New Delhi-110028

FOREWORD

Since I originally wrote *Secrets of Mind Power*, back in 1961, my books on memory training have become and are best sellers; they have been translated into as many as eighteen languages. My first book on the subject, *How To Develop A Super-Power Memory*, first appeared in 1957 and is still selling — along with some of my later books on the subject. *Secrets of Mind Power* was my second book. I'm leaving most of it exactly as originally written. I've updated it a bit, and added some material. It's interesting that the thoughts I had and recorded those thirty years ago still hold up, are still relevant, today.

The fact that my memory books continue to sell proves something I've always known — that people from all walks of life, in every field of endeavor, are interested in improving themselves and organizing their minds.

In my opinion and, admittedly, I'm a bit biased, a trained memory is one of the most important factors in mental organization. There are, of course, many other factors involved.

It is mostly with these other factors that this book is concerned, although the subject of memory has not been ignored.

There is no doubt in my mind that the person with a well-trained and organized mind is the happy and successful person.

Abraham Lincoln once said, "Most folks are about as happy as they make up their minds to be." It's difficult to argue with that. The search for happiness need not be a long or difficult one — you can find happiness within yourself.

Yes — you can be a better and happier person than you are now!
Yes — you can use your mind much more efficiently and effectively.

5

There's no doubt about it. Just make up your mind that this is true and you will be able to use the brain power you have to much better advantage.

Samuel Johnson wrote: "The fountain of content must spring up in the mind, and he who has so little knowledge of human nature as to seek happiness by changing anything but his own disposition will waste his life in fruitless efforts and multiply the griefs which he purposes to remove."

Chapter 1

Organize Your Mind — for Full Efficiency

Mind is the great lever of all things; human thought is the process by which human ends are ultimately answered.

DANIEL WEBSTER

There is only one thing that can help you avoid chaos in business — in social dealings — in life itself; and that thing is — *organization.* Without it everything would fall apart; there would be no learning, no science, no knowledge, no writing, no creative thinking, no competitive business — nothing!

This should be obvious to you. One's entire life is built around organization from the moment of birth — even from the moment of conception. The world we live in, the universe, everything about us is organized. All our activities, whether they be directed toward making a living, or enjoying ourselves, or both, are planned and organized.

An expectant mother follows a definite regimen suggested by her obstetrician. After the baby is born, he is fed, bathed and made to rest according to a definite system. Even his food consists of a formula of planned ingredients.

7

When the child starts school, he is faced with more order, planning and organization. And so it goes, until he becomes the
reluctant participant in a carefully organized funeral. So, from
conception to death, we must organize our pursuits, or activities,
even our joys and our sorrows. Above all, we should and must organize our thinking.

I don't mean that you should organize your thinking just to aid
you in business or in your job; although that is quite an important
part of the entire picture. I mean you should organize your mind in
general — for all things, throughout the rest of your life. If you look
at life with an organized mind instead of through the proverbial
rose-colored glasses (although they have their place, too), you will
surely see success and happiness from a much better vantage
point.

If you manage to organize your mind, you will organize and manage your life, and it is to this end that this book is dedicated.

Be Your Own Efficiency Expert

To organize your mind is to control it, and according to Charles Dar-
win, "The highest possible stage in moral culture is when we recognize that we ought to control our thoughts."

Business, of course, recognized the importance of organization
long ago. That is why the business world uses so many efficiency
experts, "efficiency expert" — another name for one who is an
expert in organization. Just as it is another name for "efficiency
engineer" and "efficiency consultant."

Basically, organization is simply a question of systemization.
Have you ever watched a good short-order cook at work during a
busy lunch hour? Well, when you get the chance, observe one carefully. Almost every move he makes is done for a definite purpose.
All the ingredients that he may have to use are within easy reach;
the most used, closest to him. He is so familiar with the positions of
these ingredients that he can reach for any one of them almost
without looking.

One of the countermen may order a "B and T down" — bacon and
tomato on toast. The short-order man immediately puts two pieces
of bread into the toaster and places the bacon on the griddle, and
takes out a couple of slices of tomato, almost in one continuous
movement.

If eggs are ordered, he stops whatever he's doing for just enough
time to put out two eggs. The fact that the eggs are out is enough to

remind him of that standing order. If he were to try to remember every order as it was called, he'd be in a mess in no time at all. Any competent short-order cook has at least one key ingredient for every order, which he immediately places on his working surface the moment the order is called.

That is the organized or systematic way of being a short-order cook. The same idea can be, and certainly should be, applied to any other activity. The fastest, most efficent, easiest and best way of doing anything, including thinking, is the organized way. The short-order cook example is a good instance of advance preparation, which is one of the first steps in organization. Preparation, planning ahead, anticipating and getting ready for minor difficulties or obstacles are all part of, or synonymous with, organization.

This book is an effort on my part to aid you in systematizing your thinking. I'm taking quite a chance, too, because it has been said (by Don Marquis) that, "If you make people think they're thinking, they'll love you. If you really make them think, they'll hate you." Well, I'm willing to take that chance, even though I know that most of us tend to be lazy and become quite annoyed at having to make the effort necessary to think clearly and in an organized manner.

In this day and age when efficiency and organization are virtually essentials for success, I see no reason for anybody to tolerate inefficiency in himself. Particularly when something can be done about it! Fundamentally, there is only one person responsible for how you think, for what goes on in your mind, and that person is — You!

The fact that you're reading this book right now is your first step toward the goal of an organized mind. You're interested; and interest is an essential element for learning anything. Another essential for learning is to do something about it; and when you picked up this book, at least you did *something!*

Unfortunately, too many people in this world are talkers and wishers instead of doers. And — sad but true — those who need help most are the ones who rarely will make the effort to procure that help. People who have a perfect set of teeth will visit the dentist twice a year. The ones who *should* see their dentist rarely do.

Going to a psychiatrist has become the thing to do in certain circles; but again, many of those who really need psychiatric help never admit it and, therefore, never get it. Since my main business is memory, I meet the "talkers" and "wishers" almost constantly. After one of my keynote talks, most of those who already have pretty good memories will be the ones most anxious to go out and pick up one of my books on memory training.

Then I always get a few who say, "I have the worst memory in the world — nothing can ever help me!" Well, nothing ever will so long as they feel that way about it; and they're the ones who need it most. Then I get those whose attitude is "Boy, I'd give a million dollars for a memory like that!" But will they walk into a bookstore and spend only thirteen to twenty dollars for a book that *would* give them a memory like that? Very seldom.

I mention all this, not because I'm trying to sell any of my books on memory — they do quite well, thank you — but because I have the feeling that most of the "how to" books written today rarely get into the hands of those who need to learn "how to" most desperately. As for those who won't make the effort to get help — well, as the song says, "That's their Red Wagon" and they have to keep draggin' it around. I guess Benedict Spinoza had people like that in mind when he said, "So long as a man imagines that he cannot do this or that, so long is he determined not to do it; and consequently, so long is it impossible to him that he should do it."

You Live the Way You Think

Organized thinking really means controlling thought reactions properly, and solving problems in the most efficient manner possible at the time. As you will see further on in this book, it is my contention that most of our thinking is directed toward solving some problem or other.

The way we react mentally to anything that happens to us, that we see, hear, touch or experience — and the way we go about solving the problems it poses — is what occupies our minds all the time. This being so, it is an obvious conclusion that you might as well react and solve your problems in an organized way as in any other way.

There are examples of this throughout the book, but I feel that it is necessary to give you one or two right now. One example of proper reaction is described in something I read recently. It is an instance of reaction to an insult, and it was written by Russell Lyons. He wrote: "The only graceful way to accept an insult is to ignore it; if you can't ignore it, top it; if you can't top it, laugh at it; if you can't laugh at it, it's probably deserved."

Now, I admit that this is not a cataclysmic event — being insulted, that is. But if you're going to have your mind react properly, you might as well do so with small events as with large ones.

The way you think is the way you live. Think properly, clearly and effectively, and success and happiness must come to you. This is true regardless of the obstacles, disabilities, irritations and annoyances that must inevitably face all of us.

Pry open that closed mind, and imagination, organization and creativeness will be sucked into it as air into a vacuum. When Sir Isaac Newton was asked how he went about discovering the law of gravity, he answered, "By thinking about it." This, of course, was a true answer, but obviously not quite so simple as it appeared.

Many men had witnessed an apple falling to the ground, just as Newton did. However, Newton "thought" about it; he reacted to it properly. His mind asked questions: "Why did the apple fall down? Why didn't it fall up?" His thoughts did not stay in one groove. They covered and worried the subject from all possible angles, trying to solve the problem, or answer the questions.

It is not my intention to teach you to discover great natural laws; but perhaps you will learn the importance of seeing things clearly, and thinking of these things properly and effectively, after you've read what I have to say. You may be of the opinion that you *do* think clearly about things. Well, maybe you do — but since early Greek civilization, philosophers have been suggesting that before everything else we should "know ourselves." We all spend more time thinking about ourselves than about any other subject, yet isn't it amazing how little we *do* know about ourselves?

When thinking about a problem, you must learn to get out of the well-worn grooves. Think or observe from every possible angle. For example: here is the Roman numeral IX. Now for a little problem — or riddle, if you will. Can you add just one mark or symbol to this Roman numeral, and change it into the number 6?

You should be able to work it out in just a few moments. The reason you won't solve it immediately is because your thinking has been "misdirected" — it has been steered along a groove; the wrong groove, of course.

Misdirection is the greatest weapon of our professional magicians. If they fool you, it is not because the hand is quicker than the eye, but because they make you think along the wrong lines. They throw in a few "red herrings" to keep your mind occupied, while the important machinations that make the trick come off go unnoticed.

In this particular case, I've led you to think along the lines of Roman numerals. If you persist in thinking that way, you'll never solve this simple problem. Eventually, of course, you'll get out of that mental groove, and the answer will all but hit you between the eyes.

If you haven't solved it yet — well, simply place an "S" in front of the letters IX, and you've formed the word "SIX." People who are accustomed to thinking about things from many angles will solve a riddle like this almost instantly.

Do You Think — or Do You Merely Daydream?

Organizing your mind also implies heading toward a definite goal. If your thinking is just daydreaming, in most cases you're heading nowhere. Don't misunderstand — if daydreams are constructive, if they act as inspiration, if they lead to action, then they are productive. But if they take the place of action, that's bad! Too many of us learn to become satisfied by daydreams; they become substitutes for the real thing, and we may find ourselves refusing to make the effort or working toward reality.

The late Richard Himber (musician/magician) was a good friend, and a successful man. When I asked him to give me one sentence on how to become successful, he said, "Hard work applied properly and intelligently, and thinking in an organized manner, must lead to success."

Well, it's difficult to argue with that. Hard work is an asset, sure — if it's applied properly; and the ability to think is our most useful asset if it is organized thinking!

Professor William James said that, "Compared to what we ought to be, we are only half awake. We are making use of only a small part of our mental resources." Well, I doubt if, in our lifetime, we will ever learn to use all our knowledge and mental resources — but let us at least try to make the best use of what we have! Attempt to organize and discipline those resources, and you are on your way to a more successful, happy and creative life.

"It is the mind that maketh good or ill, that maketh wretched or happy, rich or poor," yet we spend more time on inconsequential things than we do on organizing our minds. Time is more important than money; it's the most valuable commodity we can spend; so if you're looking for a bargain, spend some on your thinking powers. Just make up your mind that there is much room for improvement, and you'll make some improvement.

There is no limit to how much we can learn, you know, if we will only acquire that most important single piece of knowledge, and that is the knowledge of how little we know!

"Follow the Girls" to Success

In this chapter I've attempted to tell you a little bit of what this book is to be about. An organized mind will help to get rid of fears, worries, doubts, indecision — uncertainties, in general. It will help you to react properly, to solve problems effectively. It will help you to replace bad habits with good ones, to plan ahead, to make life easier — above all, to live a happy and successful life.

An organized mind encompasses a myriad of subjects, many of which I have no space to write about. I've selected the ones that I feel are most essential.

One of our clichés is: "Live for today only." Well, I agree with that, except that I would like to change it to "Live for today and tomorrow only!" I believe in looking ahead, at least until tomorrow; the day after tomorrow can be planned for, and thought about — tomorrow.

Just recently, at a resort hotel where I appeared for a corporate convention, I marveled at the thinking ahead of the proprietor. There was a sign at the entrance to the dining room which said, "To avoid the carrying of fruit out of the dining room, there will be no fruit served in the dining room!"

Then I was quite favorably impressed one day as I waited for a friend on New York's Madison Avenue. The wolves in gray flannel suits were out in droves (I was wearing blue serge). Some of the most beautiful girls in the world can be seen strolling on Madison Avenue. I watched some of the men watching the girls. One man in particular liked to follow them (with his eyes) as they passed.

I guess he didn't want this to be obvious, so he planned ahead. When he saw a particularly delectable female approaching from the direction he was facing, he turned to face in the opposite direction before the girl passed. In this way, he was able to "follow the girls" without a breach of manners, and without making it obvious. Now there was an organized mind!

Chapter 2

Cultivate Your Interest —
to the Pitch of Success

Art thou lonely, O my brother?
Share thy little with another!
Stretch a hand to one unfriended,
And the loneliness is ended.

WILLIAM ARTHUR DUNKERLEY

We are all, each and every one of us, completely and irrevocably alone. No matter how many friends a person may have, nor how close those friends may be, it does not change this thought — or fact, if you will — that we are each an entity unto ourselves.

I'm sure that many, if not all, of you have experienced the dismal feeling of being more alone in a crowded room than when you were actually physically alone.

I've mentioned close friends, but the same goes for relatives; even someone as close to you as your husband or wife. There is always something that just cannot be communicated to anyone — something that cannot be put into words, or just too personal to confide in others.

Probably a thousand people have greeted you this last year with the question, "How are you?" Have you ever answered that question literally? In other words, really told these people how you are?

15

Told them about your personal aches and pains, about the trouble at your job or at home? If you have, you may have noticed a subtle glazing of your acquaintance's eyes after a few moments. Perhaps they got a bit fidgety, and probably left you talking to yourself after a while. Because, don't you see, people aren't really interested.

Your troubles and problems are yours, my friend, and nobody else really cares. You know why, don't you? Because they all have problems of their own. Certainly theirs are more important to them than yours. And, conversely, nobody's problems are quite so important or imperative to you as are your own.

Curing the Private "I" Complex

This is all leading up to a very helpful point. I've told you, and I'm sure you agree, that we are all completely alone. But there is a way, a comparatively simple way to relieve that loneliness just a bit.

And that is to overcome the overpowering dictates of the great "private I." Most of us are so firmly imprisoned in that seemingly escape-proof cell of ego, that dark, despairing dungeon of self, that we tend to believe that the entire world revolves around "me." This is an all-too-common ailment, this "Private I" complex, but it can be, shall we say, arrested, if not completely cured! How? Simply by being interested in others.

Now is that such a difficult pill to swallow in order to alleviate such a painful disease? Of course not — although it's not quite so easy as it sounds. At first you will probably have to force yourself to be interested in others. Pulling your interest away from yourself, your problems, your cares, is like pulling two powerful magnets apart — but you can do it! Force it for a while, and I think you'll be surprised to find that in a short time you actually *will* be interested in others.

It may help you to do this if you make a habit of trying to think of the other person as another "I," instead of "he," "she," or "they." I know that this is a large dose to swallow; it's a concept that almost goes against nature, but try it. You needn't be afraid, you'll never really be able to completely stop thinking of yourself; and I doubt if it would be a wise thing even if you could. Selfishness used intelligently can be a good force. But identifying yourself with others will tend to relieve that momentous loneliness.

Yes — this does involve doing things for others, too. If you are really interested in others' welfare, you will *want* to do things for them. Tolstoy said, "We love people not for what they can do for us, but for what we can do for them." Tolstoy knew what he was talking about.

Many others, all certainly more knowledgeable than I, have said repeatedly that the only way to be happy is to try to make others happy. Dr. Albert Schweitzer said that in so doing we find "our secret source of true peace and lifelong satisfaction." To my mind, it all boils down to doing something about that ever-present individual loneliness. You'll never be so close to anyone as when you are doing something for them with no other motive than their happiness or welfare.

Please don't delude yourself into thinking that you're doing that when you have some ulterior motive in mind. You may actually be helping someone, or doing something for them — but if you do it with a secret, selfish motive, it just isn't the same thing. You may fool everyone else, but you'll find it almost impossible to fool yourself.

Oh, there are many people who put up a great front of total altruism. Virtually everything they do is to help others, or so they would have you believe. But down deep they know that they choose the people for whom they wish to do things for purposes of their own. Either that or they have a martyr complex which they have to satisfy — which is just as selfish a reason for helping others as any other.

Be honest now — would you go as far out of your way for someone who meant absolutely nothing to you as you would for a person who might throw some business your way, or who might return the favor in one fashion or another? I think not. Don't get me wrong — I'm not suggesting that every time you do something for someone it has to be completely unselfish and altruistic. As I said before, not only is this impossible, but not too desirable either.

Breaking Out of the Box of Loneliness

On the other hand, if you never help anyone without a selfish motive in mind (and too many of us go through life behaving this way) you will have a tough time relieving that loneliness.

Forget what *you* want for a moment, and think of what the other person wants. If you will only realize that everyone has basically the same desires and hopes that you do, you may find this easier to do. I don't wish to go into a lot of examples of how certain people attain their own desires while earnestly striving for others. You can find such examples in the biography of any successful person;

in any book which teaches you how to attain, or prepares you for, success.

You'll discover the truth of this once you really and earnestly try doing for others as you would for yourself. No — I don't mean "Do unto others, etc." I mean do *for* others. I've always been a little careful about following the "golden rule" too literally, because it does not take into consideration the completely different tastes and preferences of different people.

Doing unto others as you would have them do unto you is fine when you know that the others in question like the same things that you do. As an extreme example, I certainly wouldn't be too happy about a masochist applying the golden rule to me! What he would have others do unto him, I can live without!

To get back on track — I think you'll find that showing an honest interest, and having an honest interest, in others will cause others to be more interested in you. This will create just a little nick in that iron constitution of the "private I" — but enough to make it just a bit less private.

From here on in, instead of thinking of yourself, or of what you're going to say next, when someone talks to you, *listen* to him! Feign that attention at first, if you have to, it will soon become real enough.

I have never yet met anybody, from any walk of life, from whom I haven't learned something. Some part of their experience, some thought or idea, no matter how minute, was passed over from them to me. If such a thought or idea did not get across, I would work to make it happen. I feel a sense of personal loss if I don't learn something from each and every individual I meet.

This could not happen if I weren't listening — I mean *really* listening — to them. And, as has been said before, your education doesn't really begin until you start to listen.

Of course, one activity blends into another. It is almost impossible to separate attentive listening and interest. If you have trouble listening to people, get interested in them. If you are finding it difficult to get interested in people, start listening to them attentively. One helps you accomplish the other.

Now then, as I've explained, you will not relieve that relentless loneliness until you can be interested in, or do things for, others unselfishly. If the thought is with you that you are doing all this for that very reason, it is no longer unselfish. Stop thinking about it — just do it. Although if you start following these instructions right now, you'll do so for a basically selfish reason, I think you'll forget that reason in a short time. Because, you see, you'll become genuinely interested in the people you're doing things for.

If You Dislike People, You Make Yourself Dislikable

The loneliest people in the world, of course, are those who dislike other people. If you dislike someone, it's a bit difficult to be interested in him. Well, there's only one solution, you know, and that is to stop disliking people. I know we can't love everyone we come in contact with, but if you dislike most people, I'm afraid there's something wrong with you!

A group of college students was once asked to list, as quickly as they could, the names of people they disliked. When the time allotted had elapsed, every student had listed a different number of names. It was discovered (not to my surprise) that those who disliked the most people were themselves the most widely disliked.

I have some more thoughts on the subject of disliking people, and how to go about avoiding it, which I'll discuss later on. I will only repeat now what Benjamin Disraeli once said: "Life is too short to be little!"

Perhaps you are wondering what all this has to do with organizing your mind. If you are, then I haven't as yet emphasized strongly enough the far-reaching power of the mind. Everything, every ability or talent for which you have been given credit, is really due to mind power. Of course, I'm not including physical strength, or the ability to wiggle your ears — although it can be argued, convincingly, that these things too are really a part of mental organization.

The degree of interest that you show toward anyone or anything can be controlled. The way your mind controls that interest can change your entire life for the better. It's up to you — there is no way that anyone can help you other than what I'm doing right now: trying to impress upon you the importance of controlling your interest.

You may think that I'm giving far too much space to the subject, but I must disagree. As a matter of fact, I'm not through with it yet. Most of the following chapter is devoted to it; and you'll find the subject of "interest" mentioned throughout the book.

Don't sell it short, please. To be blasé may be chic, but it certainly won't help you toward an organized mind. Anyway, to sum it up, when you become genuinely interested in others, you'll definitely be helping yourself. That's the important thing! *I'm* only interested in *you* right now.

One thing that I must keep repeating "ad boredom" is the fact that some people will agree with all these things, but never apply them. Please remember that applying them is the only way in which they can help you. Lots of people read books, and then complain that they didn't benefit from them. Well, they must blame themselves, not the authors. If you have just read through this chapter and it has left you with only a vague feeling about trying to be interested in others *someday,* forget it!

If you're looking for help — if you want to work toward organizing your mind and, therefore, your life — *work* at it!

For your own sake stop being vague about it; stop agreeing with me if you don't intend *doing* what I suggest. I'd rather that you *actively* disagreed than passively agreed. If you believe that being interested in others will help you; if you believe there's a chance that it *might* help you — then you must start being genuinely interested in others right NOW! You'll eventually have to agree that the end justifies the means; and the means may even become more important to you than the end.

Chapter 3

Awaken Your Enthusiasm — Increase Your Incentive

Psychiatrist: *Well, I think I know how to solve your problem. You've got to be more enthusiastic; you need more get up and go; more gumption. You must throw yourself completely into your work. Incidently, what sort of work do you do?*

Patient: *I'm a gravedigger!*

I'm sure you realize that the above is just a gag and should not be taken too literally. There are limits to everything, of course. Very few things can be safely carried to extremes.

However, Ralph Waldo Emerson once said that, "Nothing great was ever achieved without enthusiasm." Now I am usually not inclined to accept a blanket statement as definite as this one. But with this I go along all the way. I know of no exceptions to it and, frankly, I don't think that one exists. *"Nothing* great was ever achieved without enthusiasm" — adequate or pretty good achievements, maybe, but not great ones.

No individual has ever accomplished a great feat without being enthusiastic about it while he was accomplishing it. I don't think that any bridge or building, or anything of outstanding merit, has ever been created without enthusiasm. No man has ever acquired an amazing fund of knowledge without being enthusiastic about doing so. All great salesmen have one thing in common — enthusiasm for their product.

To acquire any skill at all; to become proficient in any art; to do *anything* worthwhile — one *must* be enthusiastic. Of course, since all of us can't be fortunate enough to be instrumental in causing great things to come about, you may well wonder why I'm raving so about it. Well, on a more ordinary level, enthusiasm makes anything and everthing easier to accomplish. The ancient philosopher Terence said, "There is nothing so easy but that it becomes difficult when you do it with reluctance."

Have you ever had to write an essay? If you approached it as a chore, or with distaste, you don't need me to remind you how difficult it was. If you were able to generate some enthusiasm about it, it was not only a better essay, but it probably didn't resemble work at all. You found that it could even be enjoyable.

If you are the kind of person who simply abhors writing letters, stop considering it a chore. Approach it with enthusiasm and you will start looking forward to letter writing.

In the preceding chapter, I stressed the importance of interest in others. I also advised you that merely nodding assent and promising that you'd be interested in others someday won't do much good. You've got to start *now,* or you won't start at all. To start now, your interest must be aroused; and the only way to arouse interest is via enthusiasm.

If I had to choose two words that would help more people than any other words in this book, I would choose "enthusiastic interest." A lethargic interest in anything is akin to no interest at all.

All I'm trying to bring out here is that you can't really be interested in others if you're not enthusiastic about them. I know that I have acquired the friendship of many people simply by being enthusiastically interested in *their* interests and/or problems. It's repetitious, I know, to remind you again to listen to people when they speak to you; but I think it's important enough to warrant repetition. Wilson Mizner once said, "A good listener is not only popular everywhere, but after a while he knows something!"

Are You Doing Only "the Best You Can"?

Now then, one's *incentive* in everyday living—the goals one sets for himself or herself—is closely related to enthusiasm. All the things that have been said, and can be said, about enthusiasm are usually also true of incentive.

I am not a psychologist or psychiatrist, so I won't give you scientific explanations of what enthusiasm and incentive are; or how to go about acquiring them. But I can stress my firm belief that these things are self-controlled and must originate in the mind.

Anyway, I'm sure you realize as well as I do that without incentive there isn't much success. The trouble is that too many people set up goals for themselves which are not in keeping with their latent abilities. Either that or they set up no goals at all. There are far too many "almost successes," who are what they are only because they have made themselves believe that they're doing the best they can.

Well, I feel that this has become a time-honored and inept excuse — "I'm doing the best I can." Everyone is given the same piece of advice: "That's the best you can do, so forget about it." Perhaps in some cases this is so, but more often than not, this attitude helps in setting up a mental barrier which gets more difficult to penetrate as time goes on.

Instead of always believing that you're doing the best you can, and setting up these mental barriers, why not try to break through them by setting your goals just a bit higher than what you believe to be your best? Believe that you can do it and you probably will!

Contractions are often distractions. Forget the can'ts, won'ts, wouldn'ts and shouldn'ts, and you'll reach some of those goals. No, I'm not preaching moral looseness or bucking convention when I tell you to forget the can'ts and shouldn'ts. I'm merely trying to impress upon you that many people keep themselves from success by their own short-sightedness, their easy-to-attain goals, and their attitudes of "I can't" do this or that.

You Can Handle Anything That Comes Up

Wouldn't it be a wonderful feeling to know that you could handle any situation or problem that would ever confront you? Well, you can! If you make yourself sincerely believe that, you'll be a much happier person. It's true, of course. You can handle any situation that comes up. According to J. A. Hadfield, "Common experience teaches that, when great demands are made upon us, if only we fearlessly accept the challenge and confidently expend our strength, every danger or difficulty brings its own strength."

I'm sure that you've heard stories about people suddenly attaining superhuman strength in emergencies — people who lifted automobiles when loved ones were pinned beneath them, or accomplished other unbelievable feats because they "had" to. Some of these tales may be a bit apocryphal, but many of them are completely true accounts. Circumstances may back you up against a wall and all seems lost — but it may be the best thing that ever happened to you.

When put in the position of having to do something, one usually does, either physically or mentally. I'm reminded of the story that the late humorist Sam Levenson told of the poor family that had been trying to marry off its only daughter for years. Finally, a very wealthy young man became interested in her.

The girl's mother, being an excellent cook, decided to deliver the coup de grace by inviting the boy and his parents to a home-cooked dinner. They were, of course, led to believe that the young lady was doing the cooking. The mother strained the budget and purchased a beautiful turkey with all the trimmings. She outdid herself in preparing the bird. It looked almost too good to eat.

The big event arrived, and it was time for the turkey. One could almost hear a drum roll as the daughter made her entrance from the kitchen into the dining room, carrying the beautiful and succulent turkey on a tray.

As she stepped from the kitchen, her heel caught, she tripped, and the turkey flew off the tray skidding and rolling across the dining room floor into a corner of the room. There was an explosion of embarrassed silence. The girl's mother saw the ruination of all their plans right then and there. She was backed into a corner just as the turkey was.

She looked up at the ceiling for a moment, as if praying for assistance from the Almighty. She must have gotten it, for her face lit up as she turned to her stunned offspring and said, "That's all right, my dear, just take that bird back to the kitchen and bring out the other one!"

I had something similar (being backed into a corner, I mean) happen to me some forty years ago. At the time I was doing a lecture demonstration of memory with a male partner. We used to split up the memory chores. While on stage, he would remember half, and I, the more difficult half.

Well, my partner decided to go into another business. I was left in a spot, because I had some lecture dates to fill — and no partner. I called the lecture bureaus who had booked me and told them I couldn't possibly fulfill the commitments. Fortunately for me, some of the bureaus told me that it was too late, they couldn't get anyone to replace me, and I had to go on.

I was in a predicament. I didn't think I could do it alone; there was too much for one person to remember. Also, the physical staging of the performance would be difficult for one person to handle. One agent said that he had booked the act as a double — that is, two people — so why didn't I use my wife Renée to help me out?

Well, Renée had never spoken in front of an audience before, although she had been a professional model. Since I really had no way out, I cajoled and coaxed her until she finally agreed to help me just to fulfill the commitments we had and that would be that.

We were two frightened people when we appeared in front of our first audience together. She didn't think she'd be able to get a word out, and I wasn't sure I could remember what I was supposed to remember and entertain the audience at the same time. Since I can't sing or dance or do bird imitations, I was expecting calamity.

We had been backed into a corner by circumstances, however, and the emergency brought its own strength. Our program went over much better than it ever had. You see, it was much more impressive to the audience to see only one man, instead of two, memorizing all that I did memorize. Renée added the glamour that had been lacking to make this a "class" performance, and we were on our way.

That "do or die" effort, from necessity, was the best thing that ever happened to me. After that, my wife and I performed for audiences throughout the country. I have had the honor of writing best-sellers on the subject of memory. I'm now a high priced after dinner speaker and (memory) seminar conductor. I've appeared on every national television show — here and abroad. None of this would have happened, if circumstances hadn't forced me to use abilities I didn't realize I had.

So, although I'm not suggesting that you manipulate things to bring about situations which back you into a corner, I am suggesting that you make enthusiasm, incentive and initiative bring about the same results. These three will give you the same impetus that being cornered will, without the desperate feeling of impending defeat. Most of our lives are made up of little "cornerings," so to speak — problems that must be solved in one way or another. All right, then — once you've acquired the habit of enthusiasm and incentive, they'll be solved faster, easier and usually with less awareness that you even *had* a problem.

Once you've acquired the habit, stop worrying and fretting about your problems; believe instead that you can handle any setback, and you *will* handle it, more often than not.

How to Make Self-Hypnosis Work For You

Believing that you can do something is almost tantamount to accomplishing it. No, I'm not talking about moving mountains or anything like that (although, according to James Barrie, "Most of us are confident we could move mountains, if others would move the hills out of the way") but anything within reason, and sometimes things a bit unreasonable.

Hypnosis is a good example, or proof, of this. Hypnotic suggestion is merely making the subject believe implicitly that he is something he isn't; or that he can do something of which he ordinarily wouldn't be capable.

A person under hypnosis can be made to believe, thoroughly and without doubt, that a fountain pen is too heavy for him to lift. Once he is completely convinced of this, he will not be able to lift the pen. I'm sure you've all seen hypnotists demonstrate this or similar experiments. I'm also sure that most of you know that hypnosis is nothing more than suggestion.

Self-hypnosis, or auto-suggestion, works with each and every one of us very often. We are easily swayed by suggestion, either from ourselves or from others. You know how you get the urge to yawn when you see someone else yawn, or how your eyes start to tear when you see someone else's eyes tear. If I were to talk about minor itches right now, you'd probably have to scratch your arm, leg or face in a moment. You're probably scratching right now, aren't you?

Do you remember the Ouija Board craze of many years ago? Do you recall how people marveled at the fact that the gimmick moved, and spelled out answers to all kinds of questions? I hope I'm not shattering too many beliefs when I tell you that this was all suggestion. Subtle self-suggestion, perhaps — but suggestion, nonetheless.

Do you want to prove it to yourself? Tie a small object, like a ring, to the end of a piece of string, about nine or ten inches long. Now, lay out, face up, perhaps five playing cards. Hold the string at one end with the ring about an inch or so over one card at time; give the ring a bit of a swinging start at the first one. You'll find that the ring will *always* swing back and forth over the black cards; and it will *always* swing in circles over the red ones.

Get the sequence in your mind, definitely and strongly, before you try it. Back and forth over the black cards and in circles over the red ones. Try it now, if you like, or have a friend do it and you'll see that I'm right. Give the ring a moment or two over each card to make sure it has time to do one or the other. This, of course, is just an example of auto-suggestion; an example of how your mind controls physical actions, so subtly at times that you may not notice it yourself.

So you see, making yourself believe that you can do certain things — being enthusiastic about them — can, and will, actually help to accomplish them. This is well demonstrated in the story of the salesman who always referred to himself as a "$25,000-a-year man." He always managed to earn just about $25,000 in commissions each year.

His territory was cut down by 30 percent one year, but he still earned $25,000. The following year, his territory was again cut down; but he still managed to earn his $25,000. The next year he was sent to virgin territory — an area that had never been sold his particular product before. He still earned only $25,000!

You see, his mind was made up that he just wasn't capable of earning more than that. He had suggested it to himself for years, and he believed it. So he simply never tried to earn more. If he was in a territory where it was difficult to make $25,000, why, he worked that much harder to make sure he did earn it. But if he was placed where it was easy to earn that much, he worked accordingly, he took it easy — he knew he wouldn't earn any more than $25,000 anyway, so why work so hard!

This may seem silly to you, but we all do it. Why? Search me — I don't know. We form opinions about ourselves; classify ourselves, and set quotas, perhaps subconsciously, which we rarely try to overcome. There's a simple solution for our $25,000-a-year salesman — he just has to convince *himself* that he is a $50,000-a-year man!

The same solution holds true for all of us. Stop being so terribly afraid of failure that you set your sights on a goal you know you can easily reach. Set them higher; if they're really a bit beyond you, you'll find out soon enough — but you'll probably have gone way past the goal you set for yourself originally. Go about trying to reach that goal with enthusiasm, and mistakes will not deter you.

Just remember that every mistake you make is one that you won't make the next time you try!

Make up your mind to win; work toward winning with enthusiasm, and the odds are with you. If you're the kind of person whose goal is merely to avoid failure instead of to attain success, you're looking at the pits instead of the peaches. You are one of those "almost successes" I wrote about, who could be much more successful if you saw the peach first. You're the salesman who is afraid to try for more than $25,000 because he doesn't believe he can do it. You're the wishful-thinking writer who never writes anything because he doesn't want to fail at it. You're always leaving an "out" for yourself. Your attitude is: "I'll try this but if I can't accomplish it, I can always get out of it this way — or do so and so instead."

If you leave yourself an out, too often the out is uppermost in your mind instead of the goal you wish to achieve. William the Conqueror decided to back himself into a corner when he successfully invaded England. He burned his boats on the beaches as soon as he landed, leaving his armies no escape. Then he *had* to win; and he didn't have time to think of a way out if he lost — there *was* no way out!

The Only Selfishness That Pays Off

Without some selfishness there would be no incentive. I've written about selfishness in different parts of this book, and I've mentioned that some types of selfishness are good for you. The bad kind is the petty kind and the kind that hurts others.

But I realize that selfishness is what gives each individual whatever drive, incentive or initiative he has. I've appeared for many sales groups and organizations, where awards and trophies were given to the top men. I've always noticed that these men were egotistical and selfish enough to want to be tops in their fields, and I think that's good.

These same men were capable of generating enthusiastic interest in others, in their customers particularly. Read any book on salesmanship and you'll learn that in order to get anywhere near selling tough customers, you've got to be interested in *them*, not in yourself and how much money you can make by selling them. Be interested in *their* business problems and you'll know how your product can help them.

I use salemen as examples only because we are all salesmen. We may not be going out on the road to sell a particular product, but we're all always trying to sell ourselves, our ideas, thoughts and personalities to others. It makes no difference what you do for a living, you are a salesman!

So then, let's get back to our original premise about being interested in others. Since it is impossible for the mind to think of two things simultaneously, thinking of others will stop you from worrying and thinking too much about yourself.

It has been said that "no man is an island," yet many of us go through life just like that — an island. If you have no interest whatsoever in the problems of others, they in turn will have no interest in you.

You've got an imaginary wall surrounding you at all times. You can't get out, and no one else can get in. Well, you can get over that wall only by showing some interest in others. If, at first you seem to be getting nowhere, you've got to make that interest in others, and in whatever you're doing, more dramatic — or, in short, enthusiastic. Try it and see!

Thinking of Others Instead of Yourself

And — this is important. Many years ago, I asked a man who earned millions of dollars per year to tell me, succinctly, the secret of his success. Without hesitation, he said, "Thinking of my clients rather than of myself." He was in the management business, managing people, their finances, taxes, and so on. And he was absolutely right, because helping to make his clients successful automatically also made him successful.

As I thought about it I realized that it's a philosophy I've lived by and adhered to thoughout my career. I still do. When I'm contracted to write a book, I set my mind to think about the publisher — I'd like to do a book that the publisher can "run" with, can have a large success with. I think of my literary agent — it would be a great help to the agency if my book is a successful one. I also think of the consumer — the person who will walk into a bookstore and buy the book. I want to give that person more than his or her money's worth.

Well, obviously, if I can do that, if I can give my publisher a book that will sell, and if I can make the consumer happy — then I, too, must be successful.

That kind of thinking has been, and is, a great help to me. I use it for most professional circumstances. When I'm being interviewed by a newspaper reporter, I click my mind onto that track — "I want to help this person do a good strong newspaper piece. I'd like him or her to be congratulated by his or her editor. So, I'll be really good, I'll give this person the best interview I possibly can" — and so forth. It's an almost no-fail attitude. It helps to take your mind off yourself, it enables you to be at your best because you're thinking of the other person.

When I'm appearing as the keynote speaker at a corporate affair, I think of the person within that corporation, or at the advertising agency, who was directly responsible for hiring me. I want that person to get kudos, be congratulated for being astute enough to "get" Harry Lorayne. The truth is if that person hired bad speakers two or three times, he'd be in trouble; the advertising agency could lose the account. So, I do a terrific job for that person. That doesn't hurt me at all! I act exactly the same way when doing a television appearance — I think of the producer and/or the talent co-ordinator. I make myself think that I want to help *them* out, make *them* look good.

When I'm conducting a memory-training seminar I want those people to learn to do something with their minds, their memories, that they never could do before, never dreamed possible. I want to see eyes light up! Of course, it's definitely not entirely altruistic. Because I'm thinking that way, I teach my subject better than anyone; I make sure my people learn. I make sure they're happy — and then they talk about me and my systems and my teaching for years to come. Again, that can't hurt me.

The philosophy works in any area. The best salespeople are those who really want to service their clients; want their clients — the buyer — to look good in the eyes of the buyer's employer. When insurance agents and real estate agents really want to do the best for their clients, and they stop thinking about their commissions for the moment, they're bound to instill confidence and trust, and continue their business relationships with their clients.

I know a man who runs a recording studio where he makes "demo" tapes for aspiring recording artists, both instrumental and vocal. He always thinks of the client first, that's his first priority. "How can I make him or her sound better?" And he makes the person sound better even when he has to put in extra time and expense. But, he's always fully booked; people fight for his time because he thinks and works that way.

There's no way you can lose if you apply this concept. Even if it doesn't work for you, which I find difficult to believe, you'll be no worse off than when you didn't apply it. I can't conceive of it not making you better in every way.

The nitty-gritty, and part of the whole. . .do you want others to be interested in you? Easy — be interested in them and *show* it.

Chapter 4

Think Effectively — to Get Results

Thinking is the hardest work there is, which is the probable reason why so few engage in it.

HENRY FORD

What is thinking? Well, offhand I'd say that the term "to think" is not easy to define. One dictionary I looked at had about thirty different definitions or catagories for the word "think."

From all these, the following seemed the three most applicable: 1) to turn over in the mind; meditate; ponder; reason; to give continued thought to, as in order to reach a decision; to understand or solve; (2) to bear in mind, recollect or remember; (3) to anticipate or expect.

These three definitions give us a pretty comprehensive picture of what thinking is. Thinking in the present is mainly problem-solving; thinking in the past is remembering; and thinking in the future is anticipating.

All three activities, of course, are immensely important. Our lives are continually affected by the way we solve our problems, small and large. Remembering is essential for problem-solving; our

31

remembrances are our experiences and knowledge, and I needn't remind you that it is much easier to solve a problem if you've had some experience pertaining to it. Anticipation is looking or planning ahead. In order to solve problems or make decisions, we must think of the results. Thinking of results is anticipating.

Without getting into the inevitable discussion about whether a person who is perfectly satisfied is happy, I'd like to point out that we think in order to satisfy a need. The person who is completely satisfied has no need to, and doesn't, think. Because we all have our own personal definition as to the meaning of happiness, this is a blind alley debate. But in my opinion, a nonthinking person cannot really be happy — satisfied, perhaps; but not happy. A. B. Alcott said, "Thought means life, since those who do not think do not live in any high or real sense. Thinking makes the man."

Thinking clearly and effectively is the greatest asset of any human being. We are constantly reminded that the one superiority that man has over other animals is the ability to think. Most animals can take care of themselves much more efficiently; can move faster and better on land, in the sea or in the air; some of them live longer and are stronger than human beings. It is primarily our ability to think that sets us apart from other animals.

Too many people, however, take this ability too much for granted. They assume, perhaps, that thinking is something that just happens; they give no time or practice to it. Unfortunately, this tends to form one of those vicious circles we're always hearing about. You see, if you neglect your practice of thinking, if you do not think properly or clearly, the chances are you don't know it, because you never think about it. And if you don't think about the fact that you aren't thinking effectively, you'll never realize that something should be done about it. You see what I mean about that vicious circle?

The Art Of Effective Thinking

Effective thinking is an art, and an art must be kept alive by constant practice and use, like painting and music. George Bernard Shaw once said of himself, "Few people think more than two or three times a year. I have made an international reputation for myself by thinking once or twice a week." I can't help but agree with him. Not so much about his thinking once or twice a week — I never had the pleasure of knowing the man personally, so I don't know — but one must agree that few people think clearly or effectively very often.

Too often our thinking is cloudy and fallacious. This may not be as bad as not thinking at all—but it isn't good either. Just knowing the reasons, sources and causes of incorrect thinking is a definite aid to avoiding these sources. You'll find a few of them—those that I feel are important—mentioned in this and the following chapter.

One reason is the hectic era in which we live. Many people spend at least a third of each day at a plodding, boring type of employment where there is no need for thinking—or, more usually, they don't think there is. Another part of their waking hours is probably spent sitting in front of their television sets. Here again there is no need or urge for thinking involved, usually. Or they spend a few of their leisure hours at a movie, watching a horror show double feature, leaving, perhaps, time for the newspaper—the sports page for men, fashion page or fashion advertisements for women—and the comics, and so on till bedtime.

Well, what can we do about it? No, I'm not going to suggest that we outlaw television, movies or newspapers. I don't think we would get along as well without any of them. I'm just trying to stress the importance of taking some time for thinking. Yes, I said *take the time* for thinking. Don't you think that the ability to think effectively deserves at least as much time as reading your daily paper?

I do. Particularly for people like those involved in the following news item. It seems that the U.S. Secret Service in St. Louis was receiving queries from people who wanted to know if two-dollar bills had become surplus. The story goes that these people had been given the opportunity to buy a package of twenty-five two dollar bills for $95! The package of bills had been marked "surplus." These people were told to practice their multiplication tables.

Remember that no more energy is consumed in using your brain than in just keeping it alive, so you needn't be afraid of using it. It's apparently true that life, at times, is a battle of wits; so why fight the battle unarmed? Learn to make use of the most fantastic mechanism in existance—your brain.

Making Use of Your "Intelligent Ignorance"

Actually, besides the God-given natural ability to think, two more things are necessary in order to think *effectively*. These are knowledge and organization. The reason you can't think clearly about certain problems is that you do not have enough relevant knowledge or experience pertaining to them. If you have no knowledge of a subject, you have no starting point for thoughts; or you will think from a wrong premise and, of course, think incorrectly. Since thought is the "go" sign for action, it seems likely that you will act incorrectly and do the wrong thing.

Obviously, the next thing to worry about is how to go about obtaining this relevant knowledge. Again, you must take the time to go out and search for it, if it pertains to some particular problem you must solve. Aside from definite and particular problems, your relevant knowledge can only be acquired through experience, from society in general, from listening to others and from reading.

Don't think because you converse with other people almost constantly, and read quite a bit, that you are necessarily acquiring all the knowledge you are exposed to. One important ingredient may be missing — that is, *interest.* You must have a spontaneous and genuine interest and/or curiosity about a subject in order to gain much knowledge about it. One good way, incidentally, of being interested in others is to stop thinking of yourself so much. Listen a little more than you talk and you may learn something. Another way of acquiring knowledge is to read with your mind instead of only with your eyes.

The salesman who wants to have a ready answer for any argument must know his product inside out. He makes it his business to learn all he can about it. The executive who has a reputation for always coming up with good practical ideas at the conference table may appear to be pulling these ideas out of the air, but nothing could be further from the truth. He usually has spent a good deal of time studying all the problems that may come up. He is not the type who shuts off his thinking ability the moment he leaves his office. He does research into his business; he is genuinely interested in it.

There you have some work cut out for you. If you want to think clearly and effectively about your own line of endeavor (or anything else) learn all you can about it!

After you have obtained relevant knowledge of a subject — and you never can stop learning, you know — you must be able to organize your thoughts. Organization is as essential for clear thinking as it is for anything else. Assume you have *some* knowledge of how a radio set is put together, and how it works. One day you find that yours in on the blink, and you are overcome with the sudden urge to fix it yourself. Well, of course, if you were experienced at the job, you wouldn't have to worry too much about organizing your thoughts; they would already be pretty well organized. However, it has been assumed that you have only some knowledge of what it's all about.

What many do in this situation is the perfect example of ineffective thinking. They'll touch a resitor here, push a condenser there, loosen a few wires and wiggle a few tubes. The knowledge they do have on the subject lies dormant through disorganization. An organized thinker will first try to see through to the nub of the problem. What's wrong with the radio: what is the symptom and what, from the little I know, causes this particular symptom? Ah, yes, the condenser. Well, check it; but check it properly, or have someone do it for you. You don't know how to test a condenser? Well, find out how! Once you find out, you've added another chunk of experience, another slice of knowledge, with which to think. Next time, you won't have to have someone else do it for you.

If you *know* that you haven't the proper know-how to do a certain thing, you're on the way to learning it. Charles Kettering put it this way: "A man must have a certain amount of *intelligent ignorance* to get anywhere." (The italics are mine.) There is no excuse today for anyone to be merely ignorant, but without intelligent ignorance we would rarely have anything to think about.

As far as organization is concerned, all the knowledge you may have pertaining to any particular thing won't help you much if you don't organize your thoughts, or use that knowledge properly. If you've ever tried to force one wire hanger out of a bunch, without success, you know what I mean. You knew that metal wouldn't go through metal, yet you tried to produce just such a phenomenon, in vain. If you had organized your thoughts, as you probably did eventually, you could have disentangled the hangers without too much trouble.

Agreed that it is difficult to have no thoughts whatever in your mind — you're always thinking, you say. Yes, we're always thinking perhaps, but those thoughts are not organized unless they are directed toward some definite goal. Don't mistake daydreaming for thinking!

If you haven't spent a lot of time and effort practicing how to concentrate, it is very easy to fall into the habit of daydreaming. This is simply because it takes concentration to keep your thoughts heading straight for a goal. A thought must lead to some action, and daydreaming rarely does.

You won't have to do concentration exercises for years before you can crystallize your thinking (although you'll find some of those exercises on concentration in Chapter 8). There is a way out — and that is, writing while thinking! This sounds like a simple idea, I know — but don't sell it short. The next time you are trying to reach some sort of solution, or round out an idea, or create or invent something, and you haven't gotten very far just thinking about it — try writing your thoughts.

The action has started once you begin to write. You'll make progress because once a particular thought is written, you must go on to the next one, and so steadily on toward your goal. Thinking without serious concentration or writing is too ephemeral, too vague to do much good. So, to paraphrase G. D. Boardman. "In order to reap an act, sow a thought."

Prejudice: Believing What You Want To Believe

Of course, it is important to realize that man has been a victim of his emotions since long before he was able to think. These emotions, of anger, frustration, pleasure and fear, are too deep-seated to be pushed aside completely or easily. But you must try to think with your mind and not with your emotions. Our emotions are what cause us to be suggestible; they make us prisoners of prejudice and habit. We are all prejudiced in many ways, and our prejudices must inevitably lead, mold and distort our thinking.

"Prejudice" means what it sounds like — to "pre-judge" someone or something unfavorably. Nowadays, the word "prejudice" is frequently used as a synonym for "intolerance," whereas, "intolerant" is often used as another way of saying that someone is "bigoted," usually in a religious or racial sense. No matter which word is used, it still means that he who thinks along those lines is thinking ineffectively.

However, I have used "prejudice" here in its dictionary meaning. Don't prejudge anything (it's tough enough to judge correctly when you have all the facts) if you wish to keep moving toward the goal of an organized mind.

I am not suggesting that we get rid of our emotions entirely. Not only is that impossible; it is undesirable. If we had no emotions, we would resemble the characters you read about in science fiction stories — just thinking machines.

No, we cannot get rid of our emotions, but we can learn to master them or hold them in check. Stop thinking emotionally, and you may stop thinking in extremes. If you should meet one foolish woman, and think, "What fools women are," you're thinking in extremes. If you say of an acquaintance, "He's the worst card player in the world," you're thinking in extremes. If you fail with something on the first try, and say, "I'll never be able to accomplish that" — well, besides being negative thinking, it's also extreme. Thinking in extremes is, in most cases, emotional and prejudiced thinking.

While on the subject of prejudices and emotions in thinking, we cannot possibly go on without mentioning rationalization. We all rationalize, and always will, probably, but if we realize that we are doing it, that may help to lessen it.

If you've ever heard a man speak of golf as a "silly game, where grown men waste their time knocking about a silly little white ball," then you can be sure that he is not a good golfer. If he is bald, and sensitive about it, he may rationalize by believing fictions such as: the higher the forehead, the more intelligent the person (How intelligent can you get?) — or that if one thinks a lot the brain enlarges and forces out the hair (Albert Einstein had a full head of hair when he died), and other ridiculous theories. (Back in 1961, when I originally wrote this book, I said, "You probably realize by now that I'm doing a bit of rationalizing myself—I have a full head of hair; at this moment anyway." That, unfortunately, has changed.)

On the other hand, if a woman says she thinks bald-headed men are better lovers, or kinder or more considerate, you have a safe bet that she's married to a bald-headed man, and wishes he still had his hair.

Most of us will not stand for any criticism directed at our relations or close friends. We will give all kinds of reasons to justify their improper actions. Now I'm not implying that this is wrong; just that such thinking is not particularly conducive to seeing or believing the truth.

Of course, we always recognize when others ascribe false motives to their actions or beliefs more readily than when we do it ourselves. Rationalization is really just a way of feeding our egos, and a little bit of it can't do any great harm.

Now, the realization that we are prejudiced and suggestible and tend to rationalize our motives should, and will, lead to clearer and more effective thinking. One leads to the other. Your efforts toward clearer thinking will help to do away with some of your prejudices; and realizing you have prejudices will lead toward clearer thinking.

It is inevitable that most of us have a tendency to believe what we desire to believe. If you always keep in mind that prejudice is really just wanting something to be true whether it is or not, you're well on your way to breaking its bonds.

Breaking Bad Thought Habit Patterns

The next thing you've got to consider is getting rid of some of your lifelong thinking habits. Many of your thoughts fall into certain patterns only because you've allowed them to do so most of your life. Just because you have thought for years that some facts(?) are true does not make them necessarily so. Being naturally lazy and always looking for the easy way, many of us believe too many things without ever really thinking about them, or checking them. Robert Leavitt said, "People don't ask for facts in making up their minds. They would rather have one good, soul-satisfying emotion than a dozen facts."

One of the standard clichés is, if an eating place advertises "home cooking" then it must serve good food, but it stands to reason that the chef in any first-class restaurant (that does not serve home cooking) certainly should be a better cook than most wives (my wife, anyway).

After some of the home cooking I've had to eat in various restaurants, I am no longer lured by such a sign. I may decide to try it, and if it's good, why, fine — then I'm a customer. If it's no good — well, that's what I mean: a "home cooking" sign is no criterion.

As long as I'm on the subject of food, will someone please tell me why everyone has decided that all truck drivers must be gourmets and fine judges of food? How many times have you heard someone say, "Oh, the food must be good, all the truck drivers stop there!"?

There's a paradox for you, if ever I heard one. I'm too small to arouse the ire of the kind of men who drive trucks, but I think they'll agree with me that some of the places at which they stop to eat serve lousy food! They stop at such places because they're probably the only places open at that particular time on their particular routes. Such a place is either the only place, or it's the least of several evils.

The point I'm striving to make here is that we must question things almost constantly in order to think effectively. There's no need to be a chronic disbeliever; but stop going along with the crowd. Take the time and effort to examine some of those "thinking clichés" every so often, and you'll relieve yourself of some bad thinking habits.

We form habits in thinking as in anything else, and they are not always good habits. Sticking to your guns, or having the "courage of your convictions" is fine at times — but remember that Adolf Hitler had the courage of his convictions, to cite just one example, and that surely didn't make him right.

No, it would seem to me that often it is more praiseworthy to check into those convictions, and have the courage to admit that they are incorrect, if and when you find them to *be* incorrect. There is no shame involved in admitting that something you've always believed to be true is not. On the contrary, it's the first sign that you're starting to make the effort to think for yourself, and to think clearly — and that's a step forward to be proud of.

It's Not Wrong to Admit You're Wrong!

When Michael, the son of a close friend, was perhaps seven or eight years old, he had a problem at school. He was being teased by other children. It seems this school (an expensive private school) couldn't control it or handle it. Well, they handled it — by allowing it. Michael perpetuated the problem by the way he reacted to it, making it obvious that the teasing affected him. We all know how cruel children can be. The more he cried or showed he was upset or tried to argue or tease back, the more he was teased. It got to the point where he didn't want to go to school.

I finally helped him solve the problem by telling him how I solved it when I was a schoolboy. If, when playing ball for example, I'd make a silly mistake, the teasing would start immediately. I would, just as immediately, *agree*. More important, I'd make it worse than it really was!

When another boy said in a teasing tone, "Yeah, yeah you dropped the ball; butterfingers, butterfingers," I'd answer, "Yeah, I can't believe I was that clumsy; that had to be the worst error in the history of baseball!" I agreed with the teaser(s) and exaggerated the thing I was being teased about. "Boy; did you ever see a sillier error than that?! And I thought I could play baseball — I sure thought I could catch a ball." I topped the teasers! And most of the time, the teasers would stop teasing and try to make me feel better. "Oh, come on; it wasn't that bad. I guess I could've made the same error." and so on. We became friends.

Michael had the tendency to freeze when he was called to the front of the room and asked questions by his teacher. He'd stammer, hesitate, answer incorrectly, or simply remain silent. The teasing would start as he returned to his seat. It took the form of "Dummy, dummy; Michael is a dummy." I suggested to him that he agree and make it worse than it was. "Boy; I sure am dumb; that had to be the stupidest thing I ever did." And/or "I feel like the dumbest person in the world — I just stood there." And/or, "How could I be so stupid?" I told him to do just that, exaggerate it, put himself down, whenever anyone started to tease. It worked; the teasing stopped. I knew it would; it had worked for me.

Why am I telling you this? Well, if you're the parent or relative of a child who's having a problem with teasing, you might teach him or her the idea. But, the main reason is that the concept stayed with me as I grew older — it simply evolved to learning to admit I was wrong! I've found that to be very important to me both in my personal and business life.

Part of today's inefficiency and what tends to make it even worse, is that the person who makes the mistake, who is completely wrong, rarely admits it. Worse — he or she will blame *you* for it; act as if *you* were wrong. That is not the way to build good will, nor is it the way to attract and keep customers.

And — years ago when I did an "act" — it consisted of performing feats of memory entertainingly — I thought I had to be perfect, never "forget" anything. When I did "forget" something, it upset me, threw off my timing, and so forth. It showed. I finally grew up. If I didn't remember something (I probably remember more during one appearance than most people remember in years), I simply said so, usually laughing at myself. (Now I tell the people that they're in at the birth of a legend — the world-renowned memory expert "forgot"!) Audiences laughed with me; my timing wasn't affected and I realized that, in most cases, the people in my audiences enjoyed themselves more than usual, and — they thought *I was kidding!*

It's almost a cliché — laugh at yourself before others laugh at you. ...then they'll laugh *with* you, if they laugh at all.

Chapter 5

Think Logically — and No One Can Stop You

"I don't know enough to go out into the world on my own."

"Don't worry too much about the things you don't know. What gets you into trouble are the things you know for sure that ain't so!"

It is not my idea to discuss logic in detail in this book. I don't want to get into a technical treatise which would necessitate using and explaining words and phrases like complex dilemmas, indirect reduction, subaltern proposition, division and definition.

However, I do want to touch lightly upon one aspect of the subject. Practical philosophy consists of two branches: ethics and logic. Each of these is a full college course, which is why I couldn't possibly go into complete detail on either of them.

There are also two branches of logic: epistemology — which discusses the nature of truth and certain knowledge of truth; and dialectics—which is more to my purpose because it consists of treating *the correct ways of thinking in order that we may reach truth.*

Dialectics consists of three main operations of the intellect: (1) Simple Apprehension. (2) Judgment. (3) Reasoning.

41

Simple Apprehension means the grasping or seizing by the mind of an object or thing; just being *aware* of it and going no further. On the other hand, if you were to think, "This is a *round* fruit," you would be going into Judgment. Simple Apprehension would be merely: "This is a fruit." If you became aware of a girl walking toward you, and you thought, "This is a girl," that too would be Simple Apprehension.

Now, in order to reach a Judgment, two Simple Apprehensions pertaining to the same subject are necessary. Using the fruit as an example, one Simple Apprehension is the fact that the object *is* a fruit. The second Simple Apprehension is that it is round. This leads you to the Judgment: "This is a round fruit." Your first Simple Aprehension was: "This is a girl." If you think, "This is a *gorgeous* girl," you've made a Judgment.

A few more examples: "This is grass," is Simple Apprehension. "This grass is green," is Judgment.

"This is a book," is Simple Apprehension. "This is a good book," is Judgment.

"Here is a man," is Simple Apprehension. "Here is an intelligent man," is Judgment.

Now then, just as Judgment needs two Simple Apprehensions, similarily, two Judgments are necessary to become Reasoning. If your two Judgments lead you to a *third* Judgment, or a Conclusion, that is Reasoning.

As a simple example:
    This is a good book. (First Judgment)
    I liked reading this book. (Second Judgment)
    Therefore I like good books. (Conclusion)

Correct Thinking Will Never Fail You

Although there are two kinds of Reasoning — Induction and Deduction—for our purposes here, we will discuss only Deduction. For that matter, only a small part of Deduction. Logic is an art and a science, and if you're interested in going into it more deeply, there are many good books on the subject, as I'm sure you already know.

The part of Deduction I want to discuss is the Syllogism. The syllogism is the expression of the act of deductive reasoning. It is an inference by which we derive a new judgment or conclusion from two other judgments from which it necessarily follows, as explained above.

It is also a form of thinking and reasoning that all of us use constantly in everyday living; most of us without realizing that we are doing so. It is a form of thinking that can, and, very often does, lead us astray.

First, let me give you an example of just what a syllogism is:

1. All men are mortal.
2. Socrates is a man.
3. Therefore Socrates is mortal.

This seems to be the standard example used in most books on logic. Basically, it's a matter of thinking that because this and this is true so and so is also true (the two judgments leading to a conclusion). They are always formed of three separate steps, although we usually tend to think of the first two steps as one; and sometimes of all three as one.

Even though we don't realize we're using them, we do so constantly, and if not utilized properly, they can lead to fallacious thinking or reasoning.

They can be the harbingers of false premise; the mistake of using an instance to prove a generalization, and the most common error of substituting *all* for *some*. With a little thought, you can think of an example of each of these. Your reasoning and thinking ability may be quite correct, but will still lead you to a false conclusion.

To give an example:

1. Soups are always served hot.
2. Vichysoisse is a soup.
3. Therefore vichysoisse is always served hot.

The reasoning in this example is fine, yet the conclusion is incorrect, simply because the original premise, the starting point of the thinking, is false. Soups are *not* always served hot and, as a matter of fact, vichysoisse is served cold. Of course, this type of syllogism brings us back to a form of prejudging; making up our minds about a class of things from one instance.

You can also reach an incorrect conclusion even if your original premise is correct. In this case, we illogically substitute "all" for "some" or "one":

1. Joe Jones is a liar. (True)
2. Joe Jones is a politician. (True)
3. Therefore all politicians are liars. (False)

Then, the word "all" itself can start the premise off incorrectly:

1. All women are bad drivers.
2. Jane Jones is a woman.
3. Therefore Jane Jones is a bad driver.

Well, she may be; on the other hand, she may be an expert driver.

How Straight Is Your Thinking?

Don't say that you never think in any of these grooves. Most of us do. The "home cooking" and "truck driver stops" mentioned in the preceding chapter are good examples of it. And how many times have you seen a red glow in the sky at twilight time, and said, "Oh, look at the sky; it's going to be a lovely day tomorrow"? See what I mean? The false premise is that every time there's a red sky at sunset a lovely day must follow, The same goes for cloudy skies — they do not necessarily bring rain.

Even if your syllogistic thinking brings you to a correct conclusion, your reasoning may still be undependable. For example, if you reasoned:

1. All animals are carnivorous.
2. Dogs are animals.
3. Therefore dogs are carnivorous.

You would have arrived at a true fact — dogs *are* carnivorous. But your thinking would have been cloudy, since the premise is incorrect. *All* animals are not carnivorous, as you well know.

That's one of the problems inherent in organized thinking. When you're thinking of facts that you know definitely, it's difficult to fall into a syllogistic trap, so to speak. When the bits and ideas of your thinking are fairly new things, not so familiar to you — that's when you've got to keep your guard up. As an example of what I mean, look at the following two syllogisms — and answer these questions: Which of these two is obviously incorrect thinking? Are they both incorrect? If so, which one did you realize was incorrect immediately?

1. All X's are Y's.
2. All Z's are Y's.
3. Therefore some X's are Z's.

1. All dogs are animals.
2. All cats are animals.
3. Therefore some dogs are cats.

If you haven't already realized it, both these syllogisms are exactly the same. Of course, you knew that the second one was incorrect as soon as you read the third part of it. But didn't it take just a little more time to decide about the first syllogism? If it did, you understand the point I'm trying to make.

Dogs and cats are familiar to you; you know what they are. The letters represented things that you weren't sure of; they could stand for anything actually, even things that would make the conclusion of the syllogism correct — but the thinking would still be faulty.

So, if you are using syllogistic thinking or reasoning, try to check the facts and information, and make an effort to understand the component parts of the syllogism.

Again, you may feel that these are trivial examples, and I agree. Yet I have no choice but to use them. I have no way of looking into your mind and knowing your particular problems or thoughts, so that I may use them as examples. My desire is to show you a process simply. Once you understand it, it's up to you to apply it to your way of thinking and to your individual problems.

Are You Swayed by Mass Advertising?

A chapter ago, I expressed the thought that it's a good idea to question things almost constantly. Don't take things for granted, or as truisms, just because you hear them proclaimed loudly, repetitiously, and from people or sources that you've been made to believe are incapable of stating anything but facts. Robert Lynd has said, "It is easier to believe a lie that one has heard a thousand times than to believe a fact that one has never heard before." Also, if the lie that is heard so often is big enough, the tendency to believe it is even stronger.

This is exemplified by our modern advertising trends. Some beer companies are the biggest offenders; they use all three techniques — repetition, loudness and seemingly unimpeachable sources. Perhaps it's my imagination, but I'm almost certain that the volume of my television or radio goes higher each time a beer (or any other) commercial comes on.

Certainly there is no need to prove the repetition to you. The fact that many of the phrases and tunes in commercials become part of our language — and are hummed constantly by people on the street — is proof enough.

Using a "big name" source has long been a standby of some advertising companies. Millions of dollars are spent annually to pay famous personalities to allow themselves to be connected with various and sundry products.

The syllogistic way of thinking brings people illogically to the conclusion hoped for by the advertisers:

1. Joe Jones is a famous movie star.
2. Joe Jones smokes Brand X cigarettes.
3. Therefore Brand X must be a very good cigarette.

Why? Why do people allow themselves to think this way when obviously the only part of the syllogism that they know is true is the first part of it? Certainly we are not naive enough to believe that Joe Jones really uses every product he lends his name to. And if he did, what in the world makes Mr. Jones a criterion? He may be an excellent actor, but for all we know, he may be a terrible judge of cigarettes.

Well, the answer is that we all like to be led along that easy-to-travel path of least resistance. I have no bones to pick with the advertising companies. They are doing their job, and doing it well. Also, I have no quarrel with the manufacturers of the products. They want to sell as much of their products as they can — and if the type of commercials mentioned here didn't sell them, they wouldn't be on the air.

So don't misconstrue me. The commercials are okay with me — but don't let them fog your thinking. You've heard or seen commercials for perhaps ten different beers that claim to be the largest seller in the country. Now it shouldn't take too much reasoning to realize that this is impossible. Only one brand can be *the* largest-selling brand.

Some of the toothpaste commercials involve a man in a white jacket, which suggests that he is a doctor or dentist. He has tested them all, mind you, and Brand X is best. Do you honestly believe that all these men are dentists or doctors? If they are, would they spend all their time testing toothpaste? And if they do, shouldn't they get together and check their testing methods and equipment, since they all come up with different results?

One of the more recent advertising brainstorms has been to hammer home the idea that such and such a product is the only one to contain the new chemical XYZ. (It was "recent" in 1961, when I first wrote this — it still prevails.) This chemical makes this product the outstanding one in its group. Of course, many advertised products have one secret chemical or other. Don't you think that if these chemicals or secret ingredients really were so advantageous, the competitors would get it into their products, too? As far as I know, chemicals are in the public domain, and any manufacturer can use them. And, every manufacturer has qualified chemists who can surely smoke out that secret ingredient.

Years ago, some toothpaste companies were screaming that their pastes did not contain any abrasives whatsoever. I remember my dentist laughing about this and telling me that if your toothpaste contains no abrasives at all, you may as well brush your teeth with sour cream. It's the abrasives that clean the teeth, removing the foreign matter and stains.

A man in the suburbs drinks such and such brand of beer. If you live in the suburbs, you must drink it, too. If you commute, I guess you must have two favorite beers.

Enough of this diatribe against commercials; I only want to stress the point that it is essential for clear thinking to question constantly, and to be on guard against fallacious syllogisms. Most of our advertised products are good products, but learn to think about them for yourself — look into things before taking them for granted. I've selected commercials as an example to bring out this point, which holds true for reasoning about anything.

Increased Vocabulary Means Greater Mind Power

When we think, we are actually talking to ourselves. That's right — we conjure up picture of the things we're thinking about in our minds; and we discuss them with, and to, ourselves. Scientists have proven this by applying sensitive instruments to the lips and larynxes of people while they were thinking. They showed that these organs moved in time with thinking.

The more words you are familiar with, the easier it will be for you to think accurately. So make it a practice to work at enlarging your vocabulary. This is a simple thing to do, yet many of us are just too lazy to bother. If you would make it a habit to look up any word you hear or read that you never heard before, or whose meaning is not clear to you, your vocabulary would show immediate improvement.

If you can't get to a dictionary right away, jot the word down on a small pad, which you should always carry with you. When you're reading at home the best thing to do is look up an unfamiliar word then and there. If you don't, you'll either forget the word or forget to look it up. Not only that — it's always better to know exactly what the word means while you can still see it in its proper place and context.

A while ago I mentioned that it's a good idea to read with your mind occasionally, instead of just with your eyes. You'd be surprised how possible it is to enjoy reading and learning at the same time. Learn to be selective in your reading material — read some biographies, for example; learn about great people and how *they* think. You can always find time for good reading, just as you manage to find time for anything you're interested in. What the heck, if you're going to talk to yourself, you might as well make it an intelligent conversation!

Exercises to Enlarge Your Mind Power

You want some thinking exercises? Well, reading good books is one of them. Another is to solve problems that have nothing to do with you. Try finishing the next crossword puzzle you attempt. If you've never attempted one, why haven't you? Afraid you won't get far with it? Possibly — but you'll get better as you go along. You know why? Because your vocabulary will grow with each one you try, *if* you look up the words you missed. If you've never had any interest in crossword puzzles, try challenging yourself. Challenge yourself at least to *almost* complete one.

If you play charades when you're with friends, you're exercising your thinking powers. If you want something less violent, less physical, try the little game which for lack of a better name I've called "solvems." They're really only riddles with a twist. The idea is this: One person sets up a scene or some sort of action, and the rest of the group must come up with a logical answer as to "why." The method used to arrive at this logical answer is for the group to ask the person questions which can be answered with "Yes," "No," or "Immaterial." The person posing the problem must give one of these three answers to each question asked.

Let me give you one or two examples. The problem might be this: John is lying in bed and he is having difficulty falling asleep. He goes to the phone, gets a number, and says, "Hello, Joe," hangs up, and then goes back to bed, where he now falls asleep without any difficulty.

The questions asked, and the answers to them, might go something like so:

Was Joe a friend of John's? No (or Immaterial).
Was John calling for sleeping pills? No.
Did he need a doctor? No.
Was he worried about something? No (or Immaterial).
Was he married? Immaterial.
Is it important to find out why John couldn't sleep?
Yes.
Was he in pain? No.
Did he call to see if someone was home? No.
Did he know that Joe was definitely home? Yes.
Was Joe the reason John couldn't sleep? Yes.
...And so on.

If you were thinking, the last question and answer should give you a clue to the whole thing. John is in a hotel room, and can't sleep because the fellow in the next room is snoring too loudly! He picks up the phone and asks to be connected to the room next door. This stops the snoring because Joe has to wake up and answer the phone. John says, "Hello, Joe" just to say something — he doesn't know the man at all.

Now, there's a logical and seemingly obvious answer to the problem posed; yet it will take people who don't know it some time to work it out. If you like the idea, here's another:

Mr. Jones is going to business this morning. He kisses his wife goodby, gets into his car and takes off. He drives about six or seven blocks, then turns around, drives back to his house — and kills his wife! Why?

Of course, the first thing your detective friends will have to find out is what made him turn around so suddenly. If the questions are well thought out, it shouldn't take too long to find out that it was something he heard on his car radio.

The complete solution is that he tuned in on a giveaway program, one which called people at home. Mr. Jones heard them call his own home number, and a *man* answered the phone!

Try to make up your own "solvems," and see if your friends can work them out. It's a good thinking exercise for all of you. They're easy to make up. Here's just one more to make sure you have the idea:

Cleo is lying dead on the living room carpet. She is surrounded by broken glass and water. Tom is asleep in the bedroom. Why?

The answer to this one is kind of silly, but it still takes some thinking to latch on to it. Cleo is a goldfish; the broken glass and water are her former home — the fish tank. Tom is a cat who knocked the whole thing over! That's all.

Have you ever tried to solve cryptograms? I never did until just recently, and I found them to be a wonderful thinking stimulant. In order to solve one, it is necessary to keep your mind on it without wavering. Once you waver, you're lost. If you can learn to keep at it, you'll find they're not too difficult at all.

All that takes place in a cryptogram is that certain letters or numbers are substituted for the letters in the message. Each one follows a definite pattern. Once you find that pattern, you can go ahead and figure it out. Whether you solve it or not is unimportant, the fact that close attention and clear reasoning is necessary to try *is* important.

The simplest form of cryptogram would be to substitute the number of a letter in the alphabet, for the letter. A is 1, B is 2, and so on. The word "what" would be coded 23-8-1-20. Now here's one a bit more difficult, but a moment of study should give you the key to it.

USBHFEZ BOE DPNFEZ
(TRAGEDY AND COMEDY)

Try finding the key to it yourself before reading on...

Simple, isn't it? All I did was to use the letter which follows in the alphabet for each letter of the phrase: U represents T, S represents R, B represents A; and so on to Z, which represents Y.

Remember that usually in solving cryptograms you are not told what is being coded. You just have the coded message itself, and you have to break it down, so that you will know what it says. Here I'm telling you what the cryptogram represents, so it should be fairly easy for you.

Here is my name, Harry Lorayne, coded in a different way. Try decoding it before you read the solution.

GIZBQSQSXZ KMNPQSZBMODF

It shouldn't take you too long to work this out. The letter that appears in my name most often is the letter R. If you study the cryptogram, you'll notice that the pair of letters, QS, appears three times. If you assume the QS represents R you've got it.

What I did was to use the letters on either side of the letter to be coded. Therefore, H is represented by the letters GI, A is coded by using ZB, and so on to DF, which represents the letter E.

Do you have the idea? If you have, try rendering your own name in the same way.

Here is my name again, coded differently. I'm not going to break this down for you, but you should figure it out in a jiffy.

EXOOV ILOXVKB

Of course, they get quite a bit more tricky than that; but solving, or trying to solve them is great exercise for those gray cells. If you're interested in going into it a bit further, there are cryptogram puzzle books sold on most newsstands. Pick one up, and see what you can do with the puzzles inside.

Brain Twisters to Set Your Thinking Straight

Attempting to solve good logic riddles also makes a good exercise. Here's one for you: You're lost in a forest which is inhabited by Red men and Green men only. The Red men always tell the truth; the Green men always lie. You come to a fork in the road; you have to get to a town called "Umgowa," but you don't know whether to take the right or left road. There is a man standing at the fork, but it is too dark to see if he's Red or Green. The problem is this: Can you ask just *one* question of this man, which calls for a "yes" or "no" answer, and find out which is the correct road to take?

This is not so easy as it may seem on the first reading. Remember that you do not know whether the man is Red or Green; therefore you have no way of telling if he'll tell the truth or not. Even if two questions were allowed you'd be in trouble. You couldn't ask, "Are you a Red man?" because you would get a "yes" from either one. A Red man would tell the truth and say, "yes"; a Green man would have to lie and also say "yes."

However there is a way of asking just one question and finding out which road to take toward Umgowa. The answer follows; but use a little will power and try to solve it yourself before you look at it. Get a piece of paper, and go to work. You see, I think I know the capacity of your brain power better than you do — I know you can solve this if you try hard enough. Use elimination — write out different ways of stating questions, and see if they apply. If you don't write them, you'll forget which you've tried, and you'll go around in circles.

I'll give you one hint: A little thought will make you realize that the question must be worded in such a way as to make it immaterial whether the man is Red or Green! To avoid getting a glimpse of the answer to this before you really want to, I'll print it upside down.

The question you would put to the Red or Green man is this: You would point to either road, and say, "If I had asked you *before*, would you have said that this was the correct road to take toward Umgowa?"

Putting the question in the past tense is what does it. If you were pointing to the correct road and asked the question of either a Red or Green man, he would have had to answer "Yes." If you were pointing to the wrong road, either one of the men would have to give you a "no" answer.

Let me break that down for you; I know it's confusing at first. We'll assume you happened to have been pointing to the correct road. A Red man would have said "yes" before, therefore, he would answer "yes" now. The Green man, who must lie, is a bit more complicated. If you had pointed to the correct road originally, he would have lied, and said "no." You're asking him if he *would have* said it was the correct road; well, he wouldn't have, so he must lie again, and say "yes" he would have. Therefore you would get a "yes" answer from either man, and naturally take the road you were pointing to.

Now — assuming you were pointing to the *wrong* road: A Red man would have answered in the negative before, so he must do it again. The Green man would have lied before; he would have said, "yes" when you pointed to the wrong road. Since he would have said "yes" before, and you're asking him if he would have said "yes" — he must lie, and answer "no." You'll get a "no" answer from either man — so you take the *other* road and you'll get to Umgowa!

Try that one on your friends; see how long it takes them to solve it, if at all. Here's one that's much easier, but will still exercise your thinking ability:

You're to fill in the three blank spaces in the following sentence, using the *same* seven letters, in the *same* order and make it a logical sentence.

THE _____ SURGEON WAS _____ _____ TO OPER-ATE, BECAUSE HE HAD _____ _____ .

If you look at the answer, of course, you're defeating the purpose. Try to reason it out. The letters used must be exactly the same, and in the same order. I've given you a hint again by the size of the blanks. Here's the solution, upside down.

The letters are N O T A B L E. "The notable surgeon was not able
to operate, because he had no table."

And If You're Really Smart...

Simple, eh? Well, if you're so smart, solve this final one: You have
twelve pennies. One of them is a bad penny, and is *either* heavier or
lighter than the others — you don't know which. You have a jew-
eler's balancing scale — no pennies will be weighed; there are just
two sides that will either balance or not; according to which pennies
you put on each side.

The problem: Within *three,* and only three, weighings or balanc-
ings, you must find out which of the twelve is the bad penny, *and*
whether it is heavier or lighter than the others!

Again, this is not easy. Your solution must take in all contingen-
cies. In other words, no matter how you break down the weighings,
you must have a solution if the scales balance or if they don't balance.

For example: If you started by putting two pennies on each side,
for your first weighing (this is not the right way to start, incidentally), there are three possibilities: (1) The scales will balance. (2)
The left side will go down, while the right side goes up.. (3) The left
side will go up, while the right side goes down.

Why not spring this on your friends and let them help you work it
out? That will be more fun and better exercise than just reading the
answer.

The solution does not appear in this chapter because I don't want
you to strain your will power. It's somewhere in this book, but I'm
not going to tell you where. You'll come to it eventually....Come on,
now — no flipping through to find it! Try working it out by yourself
or with friends to help you, even if it takes a few days. You can check
the answer afterward. As a matter of fact, understanding the
answer is almost as difficult as working out the problem itself, and
you'll be able to grasp it better if you've tried to solve it, and are
more familiar with it.

So there are a few ideas to help you exercise your thinking ability
and reasoning powers. If you do exercise it, either via the methods
I've suggested here or otherwise, you may find that when it's important to think clearly about urgent problems, socially or in business,
you'll be better equipped to do so!

Chapter 6

Think Creatively — and Climb Out of All Your Ruts

The sorcery and charm of imagination, and the power it gives to the individual to transform his world into a new world of order and delight, makes it one of the most treasured of all human capacities.

FRANK BARRON

Imagination or creative thinking is one ingredient success cannot do without. It is difficult to write about imagination in a concrete and definite manner — and yet it is a specific and definite activity.

How can I teach you to be more imaginative, to think creatively? Well, the only way I know is by forcing you to go ahead and *do* it!

You've got to practice creative thinking just as you do anything else. If you practice kindness, you'll become kinder; if you practice courage, you'll become more courageous. If you practice creative thinking, I assure you, you'll find yourself using your imagination more and more.

Unfortunately, most of us nowadays have fallen into mental ruts that are difficult to climb out of. Years ago people *had* to practice creativity in order to live. Too little imaginative exercise is necessary in today's way of life.

Except for those in creative fields, like the arts, most of us would much rather exert ourselves physically than mentally. Of course. It's really much simpler to grab a shovel and clear the snow from the driveway, or wash floors, or polish the car, than it is to create the idea for a novel, or poem or to invent something — to think!

And yet although physical labor was necessary, I agree with Henry J. Taylor that, "Imagination lit every lamp in this country, produced every article we use, built every church, made every discovery, performed every act of kindness and progress, created more and better things for more people. It is the priceless ingredient for a better day."

You Have to Be Born Creative — And You Were

I think you agree that creative imagination is of cardinal importance. And I'm sure you'd like to be able to think creatively. I also realize that most people think that the ability to use imagination creatively is something you have to be born with.

You're right! You do have to be born with it — and most of us were. Children have the most vivid imaginations. But as we grow older we tend to let those imaginative powers grow dormant. Some of us go through life without ever reawakening them. What a terrible loss! Your own personal loss, and perhaps a loss to mankind — who knows?

Who knows what wonderful things and ideas your imagination might have created if only you had used it? Or, do you think that only a privileged few can come up with new ideas? Well, maybe so, but with a little effort and exercise on your part, you may become one of those privileged few.

No, I just don't believe that imagination is a special gift. We all have it, if we want to work at it, and for it. It's really nothing more than a habitual way of thinking.

Then how do we acquire that habit? Well, some of the things I've already written about are necessary here. Enthusiasm, curiosity, interest — all are part of the habit. A man who writes short stories may take a walk through the city streets and come back with numerous ideas or plots for his stories. His interest and curiosity are geared to be on the alert for such ideas. He is always looking for them.

Over thirty years ago, I was watching one of the late, unlamented televized quiz shows. I watched one man win an unbelievable sum of money, and I remarked off-handedly to my wife that soon the only people with real money in this country would be those who appeared on quiz shows — and won. Quiz show winners would start looking down their noses at losers, and even at those who never appeared on a quiz show.

Well, from that simple starting point, a little imagination helped me write a short story, called "The Poors" (the "Poors" being those who never won), which sold immediately.

I mention this only to show you how any chance remark, any observation, with a bit of thought and exaggeration can be turned into a story plot.

Exaggeration is a necessary ingredient in creative imagination. All I did in writing "The Poors" was to exaggerate that one thought. This idea works for inventions and other creative ideas as well. The steam engine, after all, is basically an exaggeration of the tea kettle!

Let me give you some concrete rules on how to strengthen your creative powers. First of all, stop thinking that there is "nothing new under the sun" — that everything has already been invented, and that all ideas have already been explored.

You know this isn't so. As a matter of fact, although I wrote a while ago that imaginative exercise isn't necessary in today's way of life — conversely, it's about the only way to really get ahead.

The people who become large successes are those who create new ideas. Now I hope you realize that I'm not referring only to writing stories, or inventing things. No — I'm talking about using your imagination in whatever it is you're doing now.

Large and small companies try to stimulate their employees to use their creative powers by utilizing suggestion boxes. They give prizes and bonuses as incentives. These companies realize that good suggestions or ideas can improve their industries and their products.

I'm sure that you're familiar with the story, perhaps apocryphal, about the man who was paid a small fortune for two words. He approached the Coca-Cola people, who were then in the business of manufacturing Coca-Cola syrup. The two words they purchased were: "Bottle it!" They did — and the rest is history.

You see, you need no bonus or prize for putting a suggestion in the box. The incentive is there without it: more money; easier and better working conditions; most important, the knowledge that you have created a working idea, the feeling of fulfillment, is incentive enough.

Imagination is what creates more efficient filing systems, better bookkeeping systems, and easier working conditions in general. And there is room for these in any business, and in any walk of life.

Strengthening Your Creative Powers

Now, then, for that concrete suggestion on exercising your creative ability. It is my contention that creative imagination is based on correlations. Correlating one thing or thought to or with another is the basic beginning of all new ideas. Also, it is a good exercise.

In order to correlate one object with another, you must use words which either sound alike, mean the same, are exact opposites, or are brought to mind by some association or other.

For example: To correlate pencil to light bulb, you might think this way: pencil — lead — heavy — light — bulb. Do you see? Pencil logically brings you to lead. Lead (the mineral) is heavy. Light is the opposite of heavy and light leads you to bulb.

How would you correlate stamp with fish? Well, let's see: stamp — lick — lack — lake — fish.

Diamond to cigarette: Diamond — ring — smoke ring — smoke — cigarette.

Book to dance: Book — read — reed — musical instrument — band — dance.

You'll find that you can correlate even the most unlikely things with each other using just a bit of imagination. Why not make a party game out of it? You'll find it's a lot of fun, besides being a good exercise in thinking. The idea should be to try to correlate two objects with each other in as few words as possible.

For example, you could correlate car to dog this long way: car — wheel — circle — round — square — box — boxer — dog. A shorter way is: car — ride — walk — dog.

See what you can do with:
   thread to paper
   book to scale
   suitcase to playing card
   ashtray to television
   chair to gun
   lamppost to bus

Yes, you'll have to think a little, and use your imagination even more, to work these out — but that's the idea, isn't it?

Now, as I've already stated, most any new idea or thought must begin basically with a correlation. If you've practiced the simple ones I've listed above, you will at least have become familiar with the idea.

You can now stimulate your creative ability by questioning or correlating and exaggerating anything. In writing my story, "The Poors," I correlated the original thought of the quiz show winners to a story plot. I exaggerated the original thought, and came up with a story.

Many years ago I learned a system which enabled me to memorize a deck of playing cards. I utilized this system for some time, until I thought to myself, "Why not use similar systems to help me remember names and faces, speeches, numbers, appointments — for that matter, anything?"

There was my correlation: from a system for memorizing cards to a system for memorizing anything else. It became a question of exaggerating the card system. Of course, it was not so easy as it sounds. It took a lot of thought and work, but I finally got it.

Creative Activity Increases Creative Ability

If you ask questions about any definite thing — questions like: Would this be more practical if it were larger? Smaller? Rounder? Perhaps upside down? — you'll be surprised to find ideas coming to you faster than ever before.

Asking yourself a question about anything, and then searching for the answer, will start your creative imagination working. And don't be ashamed because you think some of the questions are silly; it doesn't matter. The silliest question put to yourself or someone else may lead to the brightest ideas. "He who asks a question is a fool for five minutes; he who does not ask a question remains a fool forever."

Even if some of your questions are not very practical, even if you don't come up with any answers at all at times, you'll still be better off than if you hadn't tried. Quantity, sooner or later, will breed quality!

Don't allow yourself to be disappointed. Many people whom you've envied because their work or contributions seemed to have the inspiration of genius will tell you that it was really the product of long, patient and dull hours of work.

They had the stamina and tenacity to finish what they started, and that's quite important. As a matter of fact, here's a good rule to follow: Any time you start out on some creative effort, finish it.

Even if it's unsuccessful, bring it to some sort of culmination. If you start to write a story, finish it. If you have some kind of plan for your office, get it down on paper, even if you tear it up when you're through.

Many times, something you've created that seems worthless to you may turn out to have merit. Most important, you'll get into the habit of finishing whatever you start. And your failures will be stepping stones to your future successes.

So don't be afraid to use your imagination. The more you use it, the better it will become. Nobody becomes proficient in any endeavor until he's been "through the mill" a bit. The greater your creative activity the greater will become your creative ability!

I have found that many people are afraid or embarrassed even to try to create new ideas. And if they do, they don't have enough confidence to deliver them. Well, it's the usual story — don't worry about what others think; just go by what you think.

Incidentally, another interesting exercise to stimulate your creative processes is to try to make up figures of speech, such as: "as superficial as a bikini," "as noiseless as a thought," etc.

Instead of fretting over business setbacks, why not use your brain like the man who owned a clothing store, with a competitor on each side of him. The store on his left had a large sign which read, "Closing Out Sale." The one on his right had a sign saying, "Big Fire Sale." So our man in the middle put up his own sign, which read simply: "Main Entrance!"

You see, you are limited only by your own imagination.

Chapter 7

You Can Find Time for Everything

Dost thou love life? Then do not squander time, for that is the stuff life is made of.

BENJAMIN FRANKLIN

Here is one respect in which we are all definitely born equal. Nobody has more time than you have, and nobody has less. No one can inherit time — or keep it in a bank to gather interest.

An hour contains sixty minutes no matter who is using it. And even knowing the "right" people cannot get you more than twenty-four hours per day.

As far as I can see, the only way to save time is to spend it wisely. Which really means investing it properly. Invest your time in bettering yourself mentally and physically, in making yourself more skillful, in duties and in pleasures — and you're investing it the way you should.

Everybody is constantly complaining, "I just haven't got the time." Of course you have, if you know how to use it. Goethe once said that, "We always have time enough, if we will but use it right."

It's true, you know. For some strange reason, the busiest people have time for anything. There's an old saying that tells us, "If you want something done quickly, give it to a man who is too busy to do it. He'll find time for it."

I guess the reason is that a busy person can't afford to let the chores mount up. If you accomplish one thing at a time, all the chores are usually taken care of. The busy man has to learn to organize and economize his time. To him, time is too valuable a commodity to handle wastefully.

Now I think everyone will agree that organization is certainly essential in order to use time properly. Those who have no time for anything are just not organizing well.

Beat Indecision and You Beat the Clock

The first thing that has to be looked squarely in the face is procrastination. And procrastination is half-brother to indecision. I think that more time is wasted, more headaches caused, and more opportunities missed by indecision than by any other time-consuming habit.

There's an anecdote about the farmer who hired a man to sort his potato crop. The job was to place the large potatoes in one pile, medium in another, and the small in a third. After some hours, the hired man decided to quit the job. He looked as if he had lost weight in that short time, and was as perspiring and disheveled as if he'd been digging ditches.

The farmer asked if the work was too hard for him. The hired man's answer was, "No. But the decisions are killing me!"

I'll assure you of this — you're far better off making mistakes than not making decisions. I believe that most procrastinations are due to the fear of making a decision. You've got two courses to take; you're not sure which is the better one, so you put off the decision.

The thing to do is to take either one, but take it *now*. Take the first step in *any* direction. Once you're involved or in motion, you travel on momentum — you'll get something done. Remember that the longer you take to make a decision, the closer you get to making no decision at all. You're avoiding one. And even if your decision is the wrong one, you can correct it. If your choice was wrong, well, you'll know it, and then take the remaining choice. At least you won't have to decide any more.

I know that I used to spend much valuable time trying to decide over really inconsequential things. Of course, important things may, and do, require thought before being decided.

But it's the little ones that we spend too much time on, such as: Should I take a cab or walk? Should I take the plane or train? Should I buy this one or one that's a couple of dollars more? Should I take a bus from the airport or the limousine? And so on, ad infinitum.

Well, I've come across a little trick that has saved me countless minutes. First off, if it doesn't involve money, I do the thing that is easiest for me. It's as simple as that. Why bother about making a momentous decision over small things? Do the one that requires less effort on your part, and then forget it.

Where money is involved, if it's a large sum, you may probably want to think about it. But when it's an amount that isn't too important to you, and when your decision revolves around that amount or less, why not make up your mind, again, to choose the way that's easiest for you?

The amount, of course, is up to you and your financial situation. For example, say you choose five dollars. You must set your mind, once and for all, that you will look upon any amount up to five dollars with indifference.

Now, if you can't make up your mind whether to buy an item that costs eleven dollars or one that sells for fourteen dollars, stop wasting time and buy the better one. The difference falls within your five dollar range.

If the difference between the bus and the limousine is five dollars or less, take the limousine! Do you get the idea? Once you can make yourself believe that the amount (whatever it is) is inconsequential, there is no longer any need to take time deciding. Use that time for more important things.

Don't be like the fellow who was asked if he was good at making decisions, and answered. "Well, er — yes and no!"

Many people who procrastinate over things that should be done, or decisions that should be made, will spend large chunks of time on projects that are unproductive. We must learn to invest our time in things that are important enough to warrant it.

It's like the story of the animal trainer who had heard that nobody had ever seen a camel walk backward. Camels only walk forward, never backward.

Well, the animal trainer decided he would accomplish the impossible. He'd train a camel to walk backward! He worked and worked for years until he did it.

The next scene is at the circus. People have turned out in droves because of the publicity and advertising which promised something never seen before.

There in the center ring, our friend, the animal trainer, is demonstrating the phenomenon of a camel walking backward. Thousands of people turned to look at each other in bewilderment. The attitude of everyone in the place (except the trainer) was: "So what?"

That's a good example of time wasted on a project that just didn't matter to anyone. Of course, this is an individual thing — it's up to you to decide on what to spend your time. No one can decide it for you.

If what you're doing is particularly enjoyable to you, even though it is of no special interest to anyone else — why, go ahead and do it. I guess it's better to occupy yourself that way than to do nothing at all. Time can be your enemy if it isn't used!

Use it correctly, and you're on your way to success. "Wishing will make it so," says an old song lyric. Don't you believe it! Alexander Woollcott once said that, "Many of us spend half our time wishing for things we could have if we didn't spend our time wishing."

If you have a goal in mind, do something about it. Don't wait too long for the "right" time, either, because that rarely comes. In most cases, the time is *now*. Instead of taking valuable time to fret about whether you *should* do something, worry about *how* to do it — but do it. If it doesn't work out right — well, at least it's off your mind, and you can give your attention to something else. If you keep procrastinating, to paraphrase Cervantes, you're traveling the streets of "by and by" which only lead to the house of "never."

So here's a thought for you. If you find yourself wasting time, debating whether you should perform some duty, or if you're thinking of one idea, and can't get it out of your mind, get the duty over with — write down your idea. You must make room for other thoughts and ideas, and you must make time for other duties.

Organize Your Time — and Do Everything You Want

Let's get down to some definite rules. Are you always way behind in your duties or chores? Well, either you're attempting to do too much or you are not organizing your time properly. It's obvious that you must either take less upon yourself or organize your time more efficiently.

Deciding to take on less work is your problem. I can't help you there. However, if you have a lot of work and you don't know what to do first, I would suggest that first you do the things that *can* wait; *then* do the urgent ones.

In this way, you're backing yourself into a corner. You've *got* to take care of the urgent things — they will get done anyway. It's those items that can wait — that do wait and wait, and sometimes are never off your mind — which aggravate your indecision and hold up your work.

So do those first. You'll be amazed at how much more you'll get done. When you know there are urgent duties awaiting you, the minor ones will get done faster. Otherwise, they take too much of your valuable time.

It's always that way. Parkinson's Law, you know: "Work expands so as to fill the time available for its completion." If you were doing only minor chores without the urgent ones there waiting to be done, you'd take that much more time to do the minor ones. More time would be available for their completion.

The importance of interest has been gone into elsewhere in this book. I just want to mention that interest is also import-ant when it comes to organizing or utilizing time. Although you may constantly complain that you have no time, you always find time for the things you're really interested in, the things you want to do.

So, get yourself interested in the things you feel you *should* do, and you'll do 'em. Stop trying to "find" time for things — you very rarely will. You've got to *make* time for them.

Another essential is to endeavor to make routine chores — things you must do all the time — habitual or even automatic. Of course, you've already done so in many instances. I'm sure you don't think about it too much when you're brushing your teeth, or shaving, or winding the clock at night. You've time to think of other things while doing those.

This may seem petty to you, I know. But it's amazing how much time you'll save if you can do that with all small and repetitive chores. Try putting things in the same place all the time. Make it a habit, and you'll save hours because you won't have to search for things too often.

An excellent time-saving habit to get into is to start things on time. A little procrastination, in this instance, goes a long way. As someone once said, "Lose an hour in the morning and you will be all day seeking it." It's when your chores or duties start to overlap that you get into trouble. It's just as easy to get out of bed the first time the alarm rings as it is to set it for another five or ten minutes.

The Busier You Are, the More Time You'll Have

Once you're in the habit of starting things on time, you should make it a practice to allow a little more time for any particular thing than you think necessary. The television industry, where time is of utmost importance, has been using this idea since its inception (when most shows were live shows).

They always leave a "cushion" of time for every program. This is to allow for any accidents, or for any part of a show that takes a little longer than originally planned.

So why not give yourself a "cushion" whenever you have a chore to do? If you think it will take an hour, allow yourself one hour and fifteen minutes, at least. Then if the chore really takes only an hour, you can start your next one earlier, and have your "cushion" at the beginning of the next job.

I know that I used to give myself just the exact amount of time traveling to my lecture dates. We never took into consideration the fact that we didn't know the area, and would probably get lost. We didn't leave any leeway for traffic jams, or bad weather, or unforeseen mechanical failures in our transportation.

More often than not, I'd have my heart in my mouth during the last part of the trip, because I was sure I'd be late. I learned, years ago, to use that "cushion" I'm referring to now.

For the last few years, when a committee, or program chairman, tells me it takes an hour to drive to his club, I know that it takes *him* an hour because he knows just how to get there. I give myself an hour and a half. I'd rather be early than late, anyway. (I do only corporate appearances now, and most of my traveling is by air — but I still use the "cushion of time" idea.)

Plan your day with "cushions" of time, and you'll very rarely have to suffer that breathless, rushed feeling. Also, you'll probably wind up saving an hour or so most days — and you'll be able to use that for those things you "never have time for."

Stop restricting yourself to exact amounts of time. The penalty for going over the limit is too great. Tenseness, lateness and disappointments can easily be avoided if you use the "cushion" idea. Start off in the morning by getting up a few minutes earlier, and that breathless rush to the office can turn into a more leisurely pace.

Utilize all the time you have up until bedtime. Whether it be work, hobbies, recreation or what have you. If you find yourself waiting for bedtime, or thinking about going to sleep, you're bored, and more important, you're wasting time.

A well-planned day should bring you to bedtime without having to "kill time" waiting for it. Incidentally, don't overlook recreation. John Wanamaker once said, "People who cannot find time for recreation are obliged sooner or later to find time for illness."

I hope you haven't misconstrued me. I'm not attempting to instruct you to overlook or shirk responsibilities, or to take a lot of extra time to do any particular chore. Just plan and organize your time to meet the requirements of any given activity, that's all.

Keep busy, of course. I'm a strong believer in work, or rather, activity. I think that *any* activity is a better recreation than just loafing. And although it sounds contrary, you'll find that the busier you are, the more leisure you'll have!

Knowing that procrastination and indecision can almost put you in a state of suspended animation — and that "cushions" can make things easier for you — should all be a helpful toward organizing your time.

One final word: Don't waste too much time worrying or fretting about past mistakes. Once you've made a decision, forget it. Start each day afresh. Will Rogers said it better than I: "Don't let yesterday use up too much of today."

Use today's allotment of time for today or for planning for tomorrow — yesterday had its chance. As Plutarch said many years ago, "The greatest of all sacrifices is the sacrifice of time!"

Chapter 8

Multiply Your Output with the Habit of Concentration

Success in life is a matter not so much of talent and opportunity as of concentration and perseverance.

C. W. WENDTE

Just as our automobile manufacturers have learned that they must streamline their cars so that they can cut through air with less resistance, so should you streamline your mind. Learn to cut through to the heart of a problem without placing all kinds of resistance in your path. In other words, learn to concentrate.

The art of concentration can be learned just like any other skill. Have you a bad habit you'd like to get rid of? Well, why not substitute the habit of concentration? Yes, like most good qualities, concentration is a habit.

We've all heard that most people use only 8 to 10 per cent of their brain power (which is probably giving most of us the benefit of the doubt). Well, get into the habit of concentrating and you may start using some of the remaining 90 per cent.

How do you learn to concentrate? It isn't easy, I assure you. The dictionary says that concentration is "exclusive attention on one object." Have you ever tried to give your entire and exclusive attention to one object? Again, it isn't a simple matter. But practicing to do it is, I think, worthwhile.

Of course, on first thought, you may be saying to yourself, "Is that all there is to it? Just giving my exclusive attention to one object? That seems fairly simple to me." Well, I dislike disillusioning you, but why don't you try it right now? Pick up any object; say a pencil. Now, look at it and see if you can give it your exclusive attention.

But first, let me give you my definition of "exclusive attention." This means that *no other* thought, no matter how trivial, can be allowed to enter your mind. You must be thinking of, concentrating on, and visualizing nothing but that pencil. The moment any other thought flits across your mind, stop trying! Your attention is no longer exclusive. You must strive to fix your mind on the pencil, or your problem, or whatever it is you're doing, and hang on.

Not as easy as you thought, is it? Of course not. People who know anything about, or who practice, Yoga know how difficult it is. A true Yogi must continually practice concentrating on a truth or concept, and push all external things from his mind. He sometimes practices an entire lifetime before he is satisfied with his results.

How Hard Can You Concentrate?

Here is an exercise in concentration to practice without staring at a particular object. Simply try counting without allowing anything but the numbers themselves to occupy your mind. This is even more difficult, in my opinion, than concentrating on an object. There isn't really much to latch on to. But it's good practice, and a good exercise. I frankly doubt if you can get up to five the first time you try it. That is, if you're honest with yourself. You must stop the second any other thought presents itself — your mind may turn to some sound for just an instant, in which case you must stop and start again.

After some time, and much practice, you may get up to ten. If you ever manage to get up to one hundred without any outside or external thoughts interfering, you're approaching the genius class!

You are probably wondering why I'm making such an issue over this. You want to know how being able to concentrate on an object, or being able to count with exclusive attention, can help you in everyday living. Well, I'll tell you. The object and the counting, of course, are merely means to an end. They're not important, but the ability to keep your mind on a problem or goal is.

How often has this happened to you? You leave your home in the morning; you're going to business, heading toward the subway or bus. You have a problem you'd like to solve before you arrive at the office. It's on your mind as you leave your doorway, but within no more than half a block, usually, your mind has wandered over perhaps a hundred different unimportant things. Things which have no relation at all to the problem that must be solved.

So — you arrive at the office no closer to a solution than when you started out. You'll solve it eventually, of course, but that's not the point. The point is that if you could have kept your mind on the problem, it would have saved you time and, perhaps, money. So you see, you just have to practice dragging your mind back to the subject whenever it strays.

The ability to concentrate also enables you to see a problem clearly. I feel that many, even most, of the problems that are plaguing you could not be clearly defined if you tried to do so right now. If you stop to think for a moment, you'll realize that most of the things that are annoying you cannot be pictured in their entirety. The problem is usually quite vague in your mind; you see the tentacle of the octopus, but not the octopus itself. You can do this or that and get rid of one of those tentacles; do that or this and get rid of another one. But the body, the cause, the nucleus of you problem is still with you.

I think this is why many of our problems stay with us as long as they do, sapping our energy, causing mental fatigue, and making us more tense and neurotic than we already are.

Nowadays when a person has a nervous breakdown, people say, "Well, he was working so hard and trying to do so much."

I can't agree with that. I am more inclined to agree with the saying, "Hard work never killed anybody." I believe that most nervous breakdowns are caused by the fact that the victim was getting nowhere solving his personal problems. If he was working hard and doing so much and solving all his problems, he would most probably be a happy man.

Practical Problem Solving

So practice concentration, which in turn should help solve some of your problems. Concentration will enable you to look directly at the heart of a problem so that you can decide the exact steps to take to overcome it.

Take a piece of paper and start writing out one particular problem that's been annoying you. I think you'll agree with me — you'll discover that it was quite vague in your mind. Now as you write it out, you'll find many of the incidentals surrounding the problem can be put aside; they have no vital connection, anyway. Probably they were merely anticipations. They were the "might be's" and the "what will happens." They should not concern you now.

Finally, you get down to business; you get to the heart of the problem in all its ugly nakedness. You're giving your conscientious and exclusive attention to that problem only, at that moment. Okay, now that you've gotten rid of the fog surrounding it, you can start doing something about the problem itself. *Most problems well organized and defined are already partially solved.*

List all the obstacles standing in the way of solution. Beside each obstacle list any and all solutions that come to mind. Don't worry if some seem ridiculous or far-fetched, at first. Get them down on paper. Before you know it, you'll be much closer to a solution than you've ever been before. At least, you'll know just what steps to take to alleviate the problem — which is just as important.

Do that with most of the things that are bothering you, and before you know it, you'll have much more time for enjoying life, instead of fretting about problems.

I'm not trying to make it appear oversimple. Problem solving is a lifetime's work; you're engaged in it all the time. I'm just suggesting that you make it as easy as possible. I know full well that there are many things that are too big to solve by simply writing them out.

But the ability to concentrate, which is aided by the writing, will be your springboard to action. As Benjamin Disreali once said, "Action may not always bring happiness; but there is no happiness without action." Once you're doing something about your problems, in a direct and intelligent manner, there's much more chance of getting them solved.

Chapter 9

You Can Solve Your Problems — Once You Know What They Are

> **PATIENT TO PSYCHIATRIST:** *Well, doctor, my wife has a mink coat and a sable coat. We live in a duplex penthouse apartment. We own a yacht, and a summer home, and we drive around in a chauffeur- driven Cadillac limousine.*
>
> **PSYCHIATRIST:** *My dear man, what is your problem?*
>
> **PATIENT:** *My problem? Doctor, I only make two hundred dollars a week!*

In the preceding chapter I said little about what some of you may consider the really big problems of life. Of course, many small ones, as in the above anecdote, can blend together and form some of those really big ones. But no matter how big they are, the same principles hold true: Try to see clearly to the heart of the problem.

Many times, those small annoyances keep us from getting to the more important ones. We can even lose sight of which are

73

important and which aren't. So why not take care of the one that happens to be occupying your mind now? Your mind is incapable of thinking of more than one problem at a time, anyway, so take care of the present occupant, and make room for the next one. Unfortunately, there's always another tenant to take over the lease, but in this way you'll make some headway.

This applies to anything, of course. Take care of one thing at a time, instead of worrying about everything. If you've got a tremendous job staring you in the face, it always looks bigger if you picture all its parts simultaneously.

I do suggest that you picture it in its entirety at first, just so that you'll know what you're dealing with and where you're heading. After the first visualization, take it a step at a time, and you'll wear it down before you know it. But — start someplace. Don't allow it to hang over you, making you wonder how it will come out. The uncertainty can drive you insane. Uncertainty, doubt and indecision are a few of the habits we want to kill or replace, not nourish.

If you're thinking at all, allow that thinking to bring about action. Start with the first thing in sight, and you're advancing; anthing else is just standing still. Goethe put it this way: "Do the duty that lies nearest thee; thy next duty will then become clearer."

What About the Really Big Problems?

Now, I know that you may be thinking, "Well, what about things like lack of money, poor health, physical handicaps? You can't just brush those problems off so easily." No, you can't brush them off easily, that's true. But you can make them easier for yourself, or try to.

People afflicted with serious problems like those mentioned have been offered all kinds of methods to make themselves feel better. "This too shall pass" and "I cried because I had no shoes, until I saw a man who had no feet" are some of the clichés suggested. Well, these points of view do come in handy at times, I guess, if you can really make yourself believe them; but I don't go along with them for real problem solving.

Thinking about how much worse off someone else is can be a temporary relief. But, unfortunately, the way most of us are built makes us more interested in a small wound on our bodies than a war on another continent. So, to me, that's the easy, and not too helpful. way out — if it *is* a way out.

Sure, it's true that somewhere someone is suffering more than you are, but that isn't relieving your situation any. Thinking about someone who is poorer than you are may make you feel rich compared to him, but let's stop kidding ourselves. That's not really helping you — it's making things worse. It may stop you from doing something about it!

No matter how well off, or how poor, the other guy is — or no matter what problems we have and he doesn't — I think that if all the troubles in the world were gathered together and auctioned off to the highest bidder, most of us would buy back our own rather than the other guy's.

What can you do about those troubles or problems? Well, the first thing, perhaps, is to remember that one way to make ends meet is to get off your own! Few of us are fortunate enough to have someone to take care of our obligations. Since you've got to take care of yourself, what are you waiting for?

Not enough money to get by on? Well, there aren't many people who don't have that problem. I guess this is the era of living up to every penny we earn. And because it's also the era of no down payment, or very little down payment, too many people live way over their heads.

There are too many consumers who often feel that charging something is like getting it for nothing. Then it's a constant struggle to keep their heads above water. There are only two solutions to this problem.

One, of course, is to earn more money. To that you're likely to say, "That's a big help; wouldn't I earn more if I could?" Yes and no. There are many people who are earning top money according to their skills — but just as many who aren't.

Some of the reasons for this are laziness, fear of changing to a new job or new location, and lack of confidence. One of the saddest types of business failure is the person who has remained in the same place for years — afraid to make a change. This person also firmly believes that he just didn't have the right opportunities. Well friend, opportunity is a state of mind — plus action!

Then, too, there is no crime in trying to make money in your spare time. You'll be surprised at the many ways there are to do this, if you'll just take the time to look into it that you usually take to feel sorry for yourself.

That's one solution. The other, and probably more to the point, is to manage what you do earn more efficiently. Start a savings plan; don't buy anything you can't pay for — no matter how much time you have to pay for it. Understand that these things must be paid for eventually. Buy only what you need and what you can definitely afford; at least until you feel a bit less hemmed in.

Problems We Own and Problems That Own Us

One important question to keep uppermost in your mind is: are you contributing toward the solution of a problem, or are you becoming a part or cause of that problem? If you're a bloody spendthrift you certainly have no cause to complain about lack of money. *You* are the problem. So do something about that.

Of course, health is very often something that is entirely out of our hands. But in many cases it's something we *can* control. For example, we can make it our business to have a complete physical checkup at least once a year. I'm not suggesting that you become a hypochondriac, but if you feel that something is wrong, why worry about it? See a doctor, and find out if it *is* something to worry about.

I knew one fellow who suffered from terribly painful boils. He suffered and suffered for months, until the pain finally all but carried him to a doctor. I never could understand people like that. Don't they realize that the awful pain, the sleepless nights it causes, and so on, are far worse than the pain (if any) involved in having a doctor take care of it?

Quite some time after the Salk polio vaccine was available to the public, there were articles in all the newspapers urging all adults under forty years of age to get their polio injections. There seemed to be vast numbers of people who hadn't done so, and probably didn't intend to. Well, again, I cannot, for the life of me, understand such things. Are these people martyr types who *want* to become ill? I don't know, but it sure seems that way. Lack of money can't be the reason, either. The injections were offered free of charge — but people still stayed away in droves.

Stop procrastinating. He who procrastinates will gain more weight. If you feel it's necessary to go on a diet, stop talking about next week or tomorrow — start now or you probably won't start at all. Keep in mind that most of the time, in almost every type of problem, it's not what you do that tires or hurts you in any way; it's what you *don't* do that causes the trouble!

Dr. John Donnelly wrote: "Every problem of frustration which is faced realistically and dealt with in an organized way adds to the strength of the personality. Every failure from which a lesson has been learned provides both an experience and an asset which increases our capacity to meet new problems."

It's Your Ability That Counts — Not Your Disability

If you have a physical disability of some kind, I will not try to make you feel better about it by telling you that there are people worse off than you are. I might, however, suggest that you stop worrying, or even thinking about your disability. Replace those thoughts with the truth that it's your ability that counts, not your disability.

Your mental attitude is more important than your physical disability. There may be nothing you can do about the latter, but you can, and must, do something about the former. Martha Washington once wrote in a letter to a friend: "I have. . .learned from experience that the greater part of our happiness or misery depends on our disposition and not on our circumstances." And Sir Roger L'Estrange said, "It is not the place, nor the condition, but the mind alone that can make anyone happy or miserable." So act accordingly.

Some thirty-five years ago, I did my memory demonstration/lecture for the students and alumni of the Bulova Watch Repair Training School. My audience consisted mainly of paraplegics, and people with false limbs, or people who were badly maimed in one way or another.

These people are perfect examples of what I'm discussing. I spoke to them before and after my performance and as far as I could see, they were all happy, well-adjusted human beings. They were active in their communities, and most of them were members of baseball or basketball teams. They kidded about their disabilities, and one of them, who had a false leg, jokingly challenged me to a race around the block.

All these men and women, most of whom had the use of only their arms, and in some cases only one arm, had come to this school in order to learn something with which they could earn a living. They were all expert mechanics, and could repair any watch. Most important, they had acquired an ability to overcome their disabilities.

Perhaps one of the best-known handicapped people in America was Helen Keller, and she must have believed Emerson's statement: "No man had ever a defect that was not somewhere made useful to him." For she said of herself, "I thank God for my handicaps for without them I could not have succeeded."

Whether you agree with her statement or not. you must agree with her attitude. There is no other good way of looking at it. Your mind can conquer all. What has happened to you is not half so important as how you reacted to it. Stop concerning yourself with what might or should have been, be concerned rather with things as they are.

So I hope you'll agree that there is something you can do about the big problems, even if it 's just a matter of attitude. Let's face it: "What cannot be cured must be endured" — but we should make it as pleasant for ourselves and others as we possibly can. Where there is something, anything, tangible that can be done, by all means do it. If not, make the best of it anyway.

I saved myself much aggravation once I had made up my mind never to argue with the "authorities" when I knew it was to no avail. I gave up that kind of crusading when I realized that you only score your point perhaps once out of hundreds of times — and ulcers are too high a price to pay for one small victory. No, in most cases it's best to be like the individual who knew that his package would be roughly handled, so he said to the post office clerk, "It's very fragile, so would you kindly throw it *underhand*!"

It's amazing what we can learn to live with once we make up our minds to do so, or once we *have* to do so. Somewhere I read or heard the story about the gardener who wrote to the Department of Agriculture saying, "I've tried everything you told me to in all your booklets and in all your instructions on how to get rid of dandelions, but I've still got them."

In the next mail, the gardener received a wise piece of advice. It was: "Dear Sir, if you have tried everything we've told you to, and you still have dandelions, there is only one thing left to do — learn to love them!"

Chapter 10

Strengthening Good Habits — Discarding Bad Ones

Habit is either the best of servants, or worst of masters.

NATHANIEL EMMONS

I feel that a discussion of habits, both good and bad, is essential in a book such as this. However, many of the things I would like to write about, pertaining to habit, really belong within the realm of psychology and psychiatry.

I am neither a psychiatrist nor a psychologist, so I don't think it would be wise to get into those areas. However, for what it's worth, here are my thoughts on the subject of habits.

First of all, as the quote at the head of this page says, habit can be a wonderful servant. It can save you much time and effort, and make things in general much easier for you.

There is another saying that goes, "A man's fortune has its form given to it by his habits." And I believe there is a lot of truth in that. If you can train yourself to acquire good habits of health, recreation, prompt decision making, learning and work, you will almost surely form the habit of success and happiness.

On the other hand, the worst and heaviest load you can weigh yourself down with is a bunch of bad habits. These are easy traps to fall into, but quite another matter to get out of. Horace Mann said, "Habit is a cable. We weave a thread of it every day, and at last we cannot break it."

Do You Want to Break the Habit?

There have been volumes written on methods and procedures for getting rid of, or breaking, bad habits. One authority says that you've got to keep deliberately repeating the bad habit. This, surprisingly enough, does work in many cases. The idea, I assume, is to bring the habit out into the open, force it into consciousness by repeating it intentionally.

For example: a person learning how to type may hit the wrong key each time he wants to type an "e." At first, this may simply be a mistake; but if repeated often enough, it becomes habit. The suggested cure is to hit that wrong key purposely or consciously for a while. In other words, actually *practice* hitting the wrong key until you can consciously and deliberately hit the *right* one instead.

This will work in many instances. Some habits are easily broken once they are taken out of the realm of the subconscious. This same method has been used to break such habits as stammering, fingernail biting, and many more. Of course, habits of that sort must be given this treatment by a trained psychologist.

For some bad habits, however, I believe it's pure folly to use this repetitive method. Certainly, if you wish to stop smoking, it would be silly to increase your smoking.

Other authorities suggest simply stopping by an act of will any habit you wish to get rid of. Well, stopping the habit is the end result you desire; it isn't necessarily the road to, the method of arriving at, that end. It is also easier said than done.

You can tell someone who is a stammerer to stop stammering from now till doomsday, but I doubt if that will stop him. Stammering, like many other habits, is psychological in origin, and a psychologist is usually necessary to help put a stop to it.

There has been much talk recently (I wrote in 1961) of hypnosis as a panacea for eliminating bad habits. It has reputedly cured people of the habits of smoking, fingernail biting, overeating and insomnia.

Here, again, if supervised by a doctor, this method may bring results. Usually, however, if hypnotism does help, it is for a short period of time only. The habit manages to return in full force unless you keep submitting to hypnosis. Or, secondly, and more important, another bad habit often takes the place of the one you just got rid of. If you stop smoking via hypnosis, you may find yourself biting your nails, if you stop overeating via hypnosis, you may become a smoker, or smoke more than you did before. I'd like to emphasize that I think the best way to stop petty bad habits is to *really want to*. People who complain that they can't stop smoking would stop if they truly wanted to. Most of them don't. They enjoy smoking; it's a crutch that they welcome, and so they continue using it.

Aside from tics, stammering — anything psychologically caused — ask yourself if you really want to give up your bad habits. I think you'll agree that in most cases you enjoy them.

I can only suggest that you stop complaining, and start working on making yourself want to give up any bad habit you may presently possess.

Make a New One Instead

Try substituting a good habit for every bad one you have, and you'll really make progress. Every time you feel like biting your fingernails, get involved in some piece of work you've been putting off too long. If you really want to stop smoking, when the urge hits you, if you're at home, sit down and write a letter to someone to whom you should have written long ago. Make that phone call you've been putting off, or start reading that book you haven't opened yet. And keep your cigarettes out of reach.

I think that many irritating habits are retained because we don't realize that they're annoying to others, or we don't know how to go about breaking them. Well, take stock of yourself. Just stop and think of all the habitual things you do. How many of them are offensive? If you want to take the chance, ask your friends. However, you'd best be careful there. William James once said, "We all want our friends to tell us of our bad qualities; it is only the particular ass that does so that we can't tolerate."

No, I think you're much better off if you can spot your own bad habits. As far as knowing how to break them is concerned, make yourself really want to. Try to replace bad habits with good ones. Erasmus said, "A nail is driven out by another nail, habit is overcome by habit."

The challenge idea, mentioned elsewhere, can be a great aid in breaking bad habits. Set up a mental wager with yourself that you won't indulge in a certain habit again. If you really want to defeat the particular habit, tell your close friends about it. Invite them to help you toe the line; to deride you, if necessary, if you digress. In this way, you'll be backing yourself into a corner. You won't indulge in the habit, if for no other reason than to save face before your friends.

You might try the idea used by the 24 Hour Club of Alcoholics Anonymous. (I learned about this myself, after performing for them some years ago.) It's called the 24 Hour Club because they stay away from liquor one day at a time.

They challenge themselves this way: "I won't drink today. I'm certainly man enough to stay away from it just one day. Tomorrow I'll drink to my heart's content — but today, I abstain."

Of course, the next day they do the same thing. You see, if you think about giving something up forever, it can present a frightening picture. But looking at the "sacrifice" a day at a time makes it easier to bear.

After enough time has elapsed, the urge to indulge in the habit is gone, or arrested anyway, and the battle is almost won. Try this method on yourself for any habit you want to break. You'll be amazed at the results you'll achieve.

Don't give in to those little whispers of temptation like, "Why not?" or "Just this once," or "This will be the last time." You might as well make up your mind to the fact that once you do, you're back in the clutches of the habit.

So try these ideas. Challenge yourself; have your friends deride you if you stray. Try the twenty-four-hour method, and don't give in to minor temptations. It will take a little time and hard work, but you'll win out in the end.

After all, something you've been doing for years, and in some cases almost all your life, is not going to be easy to curtail. Don't expect it to be easy. But if you have habits that have been affecting your health, your popularity, your happiness or chances of success — it's about time you decided you really want to get rid of them. I çan't stress that enough — *you must really and truly want to.* The fact that they're not easy to eliminate will give you a wonderful feeling of achievement when you do eliminate them. Mark Twain said that, "A habit cannot be tossed out the window; it must be coaxed down the stairs a step at a time." And you'll be doing just that with these methods.

Concentration Is the Key

Now, I've given a bit of space to getting rid of bad habits. How about acquiring good ones? Well, I would say that the first thing to work toward is the habit of doing things habitually. In the chapter on time, I mentioned that habit can be a great time-saving device. And it can.

I know some people who find it very difficult to do things the same way twice. I believe that lack of concentration is the reason. Learn to do things with *attention* to how, where and what, and after a while they will become habits. Then you won't have to concentrate on them any longer. They'll practically take care of themselves.

If you have the annoying habit of leaving the toothpaste cap off the tube, force yourself to concentrate on putting it back on. Think about it while brushing. Before you know it, you'll be putting it on, and won't even remember doing it. It will become an automatic, a habitual, action.

Do you always leave the faucet dripping at night — forcing you to get out of bed to stop the annoying drip, drip later? Concentrate on turning the tap until you feel pressure against your hand. This will assure that it's tightly shut. Do this with attention and awareness for a few days, and it will become habit. If the faucet still drips after that, call a plumber.

A little concentration at the beginning will save lots of time and effort later on. Once a thing becomes habit, you need hardly think about it anymore. Those petty worries like, "Did I shut off the water in the bathtub?" or "Did I lock the door?" can be avoided by making these things habitual.

I know that it's no more likely for me to leave my house without checking if the door is locked than it is for me to leave without my clothes on.

So, once more, force yourself to do all these little things with attention for a while. They'll become habit before you know it. I know many successful men who can give most of their time to creative activity because they have trained themselves to run their businesses almost automatically. The small, necessary, repetitive chores and duties have become habit.

Unhappiness, very often, is nothing more than a bad habit! Do you wake up grouchy most mornings? Get in the habit of looking in the mirror and smiling at yourself every morning. Sounds silly, I know — but do it and you'll be surprised at how well it works. Make being happy a habit, and you'll enjoy yourself — it *is* later than you think.

I cannot stress stongly enough the necessity of the habit of making prompt decisions. Aside from being a terrible waste of time, indecision is a common cause of unhappiness. See Chapter 7 for more on how to avoid this bad habit. According to William James, "There is no more miserable human being than one in whom nothing is habitual but indecision!"

Get into the habit of trying to make other people comfortable. Think of their petty problems instead of your own, and you'll conquer another cause of unhappiness — shyness.

Being shy is being uncomfortable and uneasy and self conscious, and it's merely a case of worrying about what others think of you. Once you make it a habit to be interested in others and think of *their* comfort, you won't have time to think of yourself. Just remember that basically *everybody* is thinking of himself and how he looks to others. Everyone looks for awareness and approval from his friends and acquaintances, so you are not alone. Once you realize this, you'll have no reason to be shy — we're all in the same boat.

Well, these have been some of my thoughts and ideas on habits. If you've found a few of them worthwhile and fitting for you personally, I've accomplished something. Try them, use them, and they will work for you.

Chapter 11

You Must Trust Others —
If You Want to Succeed

The father had placed his young son on top of the bookcase, and was urging the youngster to jump down into his arms. The boy hesitated; he was frightened.

"Come on, son, jump! I'm here to catch you."

Still the boy whimpered and hesitated.

"Now look, I'm your father. I'm telling you to jump. I'll catch you."

Finally, the boy closed his eyes and jumped. The father didn't catch him, and he hit the floor with a thud. He looked up at his father with tears of pain in his eyes. And the father said, "There, that'll teach you never to trust anybody."

Too many books fall into what I call the "blue sky" category. "Blue sky" writing is the kind that's nice and flowery, but doesn't say anything. The worst and most numerous offenders, I believe, are those books that do little but preach, "Have faith"; faith in God or in yourself.

Now please, don't be shocked. One of my maxims is never to argue religion or politics with anyone but very close friends. And even then, I'm quite careful, because after an argument pertaining to one of these subjects, they may be close friends no longer.

I realized a long time ago that it is virtually impossible to make anyone think that my religion, or lack of it, is better or more logical than his. Or that my political party is better than the one he votes for. So why make enemies? I just very rarely discuss these things.

I mention this to assure you that I am not opening a religious discussion when I say that many of the books that stress faith in God are mostly "blue sky."

Now why write an entire book on the subject when I'm sure at least 90 per cent of the people who will read it, regardless of their individual religions, already know the value of faith? They accept the proposition that faith in God is almost a necessity for a happy life.

But don't you think that perhaps God might prefer you to take care of some of your own problems? I don't think that He wants you to go through life depending on Him always, and doing nothing to help yourself.

After all, we've each been given a brain with which to think for ourselves, and I think that this is a gift with an ulterior motive. He perhaps feels that this relieves His burden a bit.

Let me try to clarify it this way. Having faith in God is both a virtue and, I believe, a necessity. But it can be much more helpful if it is spread around a bit. In other words, I think it is just as important to have faith in others, faith in mankind in general, as it is to have faith in Him. When Andrew Carnegie was asked to explain the secret of his success, his answer was quite succinct. He said, "Faith in myself, faith in others and faith in my business."

Those who read "blue sky" books and believe implicitly that faith can solve any and all problems are not being helped, as far as I'm concerned. It was a wise man who first said that "the Lord helps those who help themselves."

It's all right to have faith that what you *do* will turn out right, because at least you're doing something. It's doing nothing and feeling that "He'll take care of it for me" that I'm definitely against.

What Trust in Others Will Bring You

In this day and age, it is almost impossible not to become at least a little bit cynical. But to be a complete cynic is to be completely unhappy. Having faith when you're ill that you will become well again is fine; but I think you'll agree that you must have faith in your doctor, too.

I know a few people who continually protest that they do not trust doctors. Well, their views usually change when they get an unexpected pain. It's those who really do not see a doctor when it is necessary that get into difficulties.

Perhaps they had a bad experience once; perhaps a doctor came up with an incorrect diagnosis — so what? Is this adequate reason to mistrust *all* doctors? Of course not!

Unfortunately, and inevitably, there are bad doctors, just as there are bad lawyers and incompetent dentists — but the competent practitioners in any field surely outnumber the bad ones.

All I'm leading up to is that one good way to solve problems is to take the problem to a competent person in its particular field. That's a good way, and sometimes the *only* way, to get help.

"Faith in your fellow man" may be a cliche, but I think it's important to have. There are too many people who needlessly worry and fret about a million little things that will never happen, simply because they have no trust in others.

At one time, circa 1960, in New York City, there was a rumor that garages and parking lots were removing new motors from cars and putting in old ones. Well, maybe one or two places were caught at it, but the odds against it happening to me were pretty high. Yet I couldn't help worrying about it, each time I parked my car in a parking lot. Many an evening at the theater was ruined for me because I was thinking more about the car than the story line of the play.

Well, I certainly couldn't go on mistrusting all parking lots and garages. I simply made up my mind to forget about it. It has been years (30 of them!) since I heard that rumor, and I haven't lost any motors yet.

President James A. Garfield once said, "I have had many troubles in my life, but the worst of them never came." So, why add unnecessary worries to the ones you already have? Give your brain time to work on more important things and stop worrying about being cheated by the butcher, the baker and the parking lot attendant. Most people are reliable and do their jobs as honestly as possible, so have some faith in them.

All this may seem quite trivial to you, but I suggest that you stop distrusting people right now. The time and energy that you can waste during your lifetime worrying because of your lack of faith in others is *not* trivial. Dr. Frank Crane said, "You may be deceived if you trust too much, but you will live in torment if you do not trust enough."

But You Think People Take Advantage of You?

This idea, of course, can be carried into any and all aspects of life. Take your job, for instance. I don't have to point out all the petty jealousies and mistrust that goes on in some offices and businesses. Why do so many people always feel as if they're being taken advantage of? It is from lack of faith in their fellow workers and supervisors.

If you are one of those who constantly believes that others are taking advantage of you, or that everyone is against you, look inside yourself, my friend. The odds are there's something wrong with *you!* You may have some faults of your own to get rid of. Probably the first feeling you've got to get rid of is that you have no faults. If you feel that way, you'll never get rid of them. If you know you have some faults (and who hasn't?), it's time to stop expecting others to indulge you — try doing something about them.

Worst of all, of course, is to be conscious of none of your own offenses — or an inflated ego makes you imagine your faults are better than anyone else's virtues.

This kind of attitude must make you unhappy at your job, or at anything else for that matter. Perhaps your boss gave that raise or vice presidency to someone else when, after all, you deserved it! Come now, did you really deserve it, or do you just like to think you did? A hundred reasons are running through your mind as to why you didn't get it. Your employer likes the other guy better, he plays golf with him, goes to his home for dinner, and so on, endlessly.

But in most cases I don't think these things matter very much. Most businessmen are interested only in who is best qualified for a particular position, promotion or raise. You simply must have faith in your boss, and believe that he is interested primarily in bettering his business.

Aside from the fact that your opponent plays golf with the big boss, is he also better qualified than you to handle additional responsibility? Does he do his work more competently? Does he do it without grumbling about it? Most importantly, does he usually do *more* than is required of him?

I think if you answer all these questions truthfully, you will find, more often than not, that you didn't deserve that raise after all.

What can you do about it? Well, first of all, forget about it; stop feeling sorry for yourself. Then ask yourself another question: "Am I happy at what I'm doing?" If the answer is "no," you have two choices: learn to be happy at your work, or if you feel that's impossible, find something else to do!

If you want to put some effort into being happy in your work, try this: Get *interested* in the business; show a little enthusiasm for it. Find out everything you can about your employer's problems; turn your chores into interesting challenges; keep your mind on what you can give to the business instead of what you can get out of it; don't be afraid of work. It was Arthur Brisbane who said, "The dictionary is the only place where success comes before work."

Work never hurt anyone if he enjoyed what he was doing. Try doing a little more than is required of you. There are many quotes in this book — remarks, writings, thoughts of thinking people. If I were allowed to use only one, I believe it would be the one credited to A.W. Robertson: "If a man does only what is required of him, he is a slave. The moment he does more, he is a free man."

Now, let's get trivial again. Do you dress neatly? Are you friendly to your fellow workers? Are you always showing discontent when you're given what you think is extra work? Do you always say that you can do everyone's duties better than they can? Are you a chronic complainer?

If you've had to answer any of these questions contrary to what you *know* are the right answers, well, stop complaining about not getting that raise or promotion — you're lucky you haven't been fired!

So shape up — make up your mind to have a bit of faith in people, including bosses. And if you're still unhappy about losing out on your raise, remember that Elbert Hubbard said: "There are two kinds of discontent in this world; the discontent that works, and the discontent that wrings its hands. The first gets what it wants, and the second loses what it had. There is no cure for the first but success, and there is no cure at all for the second."

Chapter 12

Curiosity Can Also Lead You to Success

God spare me sclerosis of the curiosity, for the curiosity which craves to keep us informed about the small things no less than the large is the mainspring, the dynamo, the jet propulsion of all complete living.

JOHN MASON BROWN

I have always marveled at people who are not curious about anything; people who just take everything as it comes, and merely shrug off anything they don't understand. I marvel because I can't understand them! How can anyone see or hear something completely new and not at least *try* to understand the "why" or "how" of it?

I guess many feel that people like that are better off. What they don't know can't hurt them.

Well, perhaps — but I'm afraid I can't agree at all. I'm inclined to think that our greatest asset, next to a sense of humor, is a healthy curiosity. Curiosity may have "killed the cat," but where human beings are concerned, the only thing a healthy curiosity will kill is ignorance.

I once saw, while walking in the city at night, a small sports car parked smack in the middle of the sidewalk. I stood around watching for about ten minutes, and I saw three couples walk around the car, and continue on their way without so much as looking at it! Well, of course, this is no earth-shaking situation. I wasn't curious enough myself to stay all night to find out just why or how it came to be parked in this unusual spot. It may have been someone's idea of a prank. Two or three men could easily have lifted it from the street onto the sidewalk.

But I was amazed at those who walked right by as if the car belonged where it was. I imagine if the automobile had been floating in mid-air without any visible means of support, these people wouldn't have given it a second look either.

Well, I could be wrong, but I think these are the kind of people who are not curious about anything. They go through life, as it were, in a straight line, like a race horse with blinkers on; not caring about or seeing anything but their own little pleasures, frustrations and problems. I simply can't imagine any of these people ever coming up with a worthwhile idea or doing anything interesting unless they developed the habit of curiosity.

People like Edison, Einstein, Pasteur and Fleming couldn't have accomplished a thing had they been willing to leave things as they were. If Edison hadn't been curious about electricity, if Bell hadn't been curious about transporting sound, the world would not have benefited from their inventions. Alexander Graham Bell himself said, "Leave the beaten track occasionally and dive into the woods. You will be certain to find something you have never seen before."

The All-Time Cure-All for Boredom

Of course, curiosity is the handmaiden of interest. Lack of one automatically kills the other. People who have no curiosity or interest, or very little of either, must be suffering from one of our greatest ills — boredom.

There is one universal cure-all for bordeom, and that is the search for knowledge. Interest and curiosity are the two batteries in your flashlight; without them you cannot search for knowledge.

American educator Nicholas Murray Butler once said that, "The tombstones of a great many people should read: "Died at 30, Buried at 60." I think he was talking about the same kind of people that I'm writing about right now: those who have no curiosity or interest whatsoever.

Boredom recognizes no income brackets. A person of great wealth can be as easily bored as one who is quite poor. We constantly hear of famous and/or wealthy people who have used dope, recklessly dissipated or taken an overdose of sleeping pills. And I can't help feeling that in many cases this is caused by boredom.

Sure, many of these people have been everywhere and seen everything; and the danger of growing too blase is ever hovering over them. The trouble is they may have seen everything with their eyes, but not with their minds. An active mind cannot become bored. And your mind is spurred to activity only by a healthy interest and a searching curiosity.

Then, of course, there are the "fence straddlers." People who are not completely bored as yet, but who soon will be, because they seek the path of least resistance away from anything they can't grasp or understand. I'm thinking of the sort of people who will watch a performer at a carnival levitate himself off the ground, or cause an elephant to vanish, and say, "Aah, it's all done with mirrors!" and then forget about it.

Well, again, these are not earth-shaking situations. I'm not suggesting that such people study how to become carnival performers or magicians, but I don't believe that any person with a normal and general interest or curiosity should simply dismiss such events. At least keep them open for discussion. If the magic feats were discussed with an open mind, the spectators would probably come close to reaching the correct modus operandi. Whether they did or not is not important. What is important is that they would be exercising their curiosity and interest, and in so doing, also exercising their imagination and thinking ability.

In my own particular field, I've come across many people who brush things off too lightly. To give you an example, I'll have to risk being called immodest, and tell you a little of what I do during one of my memory lecture demonstrations (as of thirty years ago).

For one thing, I meet everybody in my audience once, prior to my performance. Then during my talk, I ask the entire audience to stand. I then call them all by name, pointing to each person as I do so. I memorize objects and hiding places decided upon by individuals; remember a complete deck of cards in order after shuffling; memorize an entire magazine, the populations of all the states and many other feats of memory.

Suffice it to say that during one performance I probably remember more than most people do in a year, or perhaps a lifetime. Through the years, I've had people come up with some lulus of explanations as to how I do it. I suppose they just didn't want to believe that I had a trained memory, which is the only and easiest way to do what I do. I've had people accuse me of using Dick Tracy wrist radios, hidden microphones and hidden cameras. One woman even had the idea that my wife, Renée (she doesn't appear with me anymore — hasn't for almost twenty-five years), was coding to me by clicking her fingernails! Of course, this woman didn't bother to explain how my wife could have remembered all the information to transmit to me by code.

Once, after I had finished a demonstration, a gentleman approached me, and said, "Mr. Lorayne, I think I know how you do it." I asked, "How?" and he replied, "You've got a good memory!"

That was all there was to it, so far as he was concerned. He probably forgot the whole thing immediately.

Well, now, I'm not trying to imply that he should have fawned all over me, or anything like that. It's just that most people, after seeing me work, are curious as to how I obtained my powers of recollection; they've never seen anything like it before, perhaps, and they're interested. Many of them will question me as to how they can go about improving their poor memories.

The point I'd like to stress is that many of those who were interested did eventually better their supposedly bad memories, just because they were interested and curious enough to ask about something they didn't understand. *You* were curious and interested enough to buy this book, so you'll find that you can better *your* memory when you read Chapters 15 and 16.

Take Off Those Blinkers and See the World

This perhaps immodest reference to myself and my trained memory demonstrates what I'm trying to impress upon you. For goodness sake, get those blinkers off! Don't take everything you see and hear and feel for granted. Stop every once in awhile along the way — open your mind instead of closing it to something you don't quite understand. Take perhaps only one moment to explore it, out of curiosity, and you may open up completely new interests for yourself.

Almost everyone agrees that children learn everything faster and better than adults. Some argue that it is imitation, and not really learning, others that children learn more easily because they have more room to store away facts. Well, explain it as you will, they certainly pick up languages, for example, very quickly when they're only infants.

Without having made a study of the subject, I would be inclined to think that we learn more from infancy to adolescence than we do during the rest of our lives.

I have rarely met a child who was really bored. They may be for short periods of time, but not long enough to matter. They are fast learners because they are the most curious little rascals in existence. If you're the parent of a young child, I'm sure you know this by now. Curiosity is one of the definite characteristics of a vigorous mind, and children have vigorous, active minds.

Unfortunately, as we grow older and more cynical, we tend to lose that all-important curiosity. If this has happened to you, it's your own fault and you'll have to find it again all by yourself.

Just try it. Awaken your curiosity, spur your interest and you'll push that old "debbil" boredom into the background!

The problem here is a usual one. Those of you who already have an active curiosity and are interested in many things will probably agree with me, and go on being curious and interested. You don't need any help, in this case. But most of you who do need that help, those of you who haven't that active curiosity, will be thinking, "Well, this may be sound advice, but I'm just not, and never have been, a curious person. How can I change now?"

Well, now, cut that out! Replace that negative thought with the positive one: "I haven't been a curious person up to now, but I shall practice being one." And practice can do it, too. As with anything else, you'll find that after forcing yourself to be curious about things for a while you will be — automatically.

You may be surprised to find that new worlds will be opening for you. New interests can be lasting interests and, as you know, this can lead to the acquisition of valuable knowledge.

Curiosity has led men into hobbies which have lasted a lifetime. Many of these hobbies have turned into well- paying and interesting businesses. Stop belittling those who are interested in stamp collecting, hobby railroading, photography, magic, and other worldwide hobbies. Look into them yourself; a little curiosity will show you why they engage the interest of so many others, and may even lead to your own interest and enjoyment.

Not only will a hobby help alleviate boredom, but it's a wonderful, creative exercise. It will keep your mind sharp and clear. John Mason Brown has suggested that a hobby is an "all-important refueler of the tired mind. It offers rest and stimulation simultaneously." And anyone who has a hobby or two will surely say "amen" to that.

Practical Hints to Waken Anybody's Curiosity

Well, I've tried to convince you of the importance of being curious, and I sincerely hope I've succeeded. But I don't want to close this chapter until I've given you some definite and practical advice about curiosity.

If you are entertaining even a fleeting thought that goes something like this: "Well, now I know it's to my advantage to be curious. But curious about what? Am I to try to develop an interest in every little thing I see or hear? Must I stop to examine everything I ever come across?" — then I haven't quite reached you.

No, of course you needn't stop to examine everything. Selectivity is essential, and before you know it, your mind will seek out only the things that are of importance to you.

One of the largest businesses in New York City is the garment industry. Perhaps 30 per cent of the successful operators in this business have come up from the lowest ranks. Many of them have had little formal education or training, but it was their curiosity and interest, urging them toward ambitious goals, that elevated them to their present positions.

To give one concrete example: One man I know spent a few years in the "garment center" pushing and pulling racks of dresses through the crowded streets. Now many of those who push these racks or hand trucks can't see past the front of the truck. They are interested in only one thing — getting the dresses from one place to the next. That's their job, and what else is there to think about?

But the man I'm talking about happened to be of a curious nature. He was interested in the dresses he transported. He learned their prices, and wondered why they were priced so high. During his spare time he went about finding out how much the material per dress was worth. He learned why manufacturing the dresses was so costly; and thought about methods to cut down this cost. In short, he learned all he could about the business from his position behind a hand truck.

I'm not trying to convince you that he did all this in a matter of weeks. It covered some years — but when the opportunity to go into business for himself arrived, he was ready. His ideas on lower manufacturing costs, and therefore lower prices for the same quality merchandise, couldn't help but make him a success. He is now hiring many people to push *his* hand trucks around; and these people would have the same opportunity he had, if they would just exercise the same curiosity.

The remarks in this chapter have been directed to people of all ages. But the happiest and youngest elderly people I know are those whose curiosity is still sharp and searching. Boredom makes people old before their time; curiosity, you'll find, is the best substitute for the mythical "fountain of youth." Perhaps that was what Harry Emerson Fosdick meant when he said, "The art of retirement is not to retire from something but to retire *to* something."

You'll be happier and most likely live longer if you spur your interest and keep your curiosity at a keen edge. To those people whose curiosity has caused them to be interested in many things, the world is full of satisfaction. When you lose interest you begin to grow old instead of older. I really believe that people with a healthy curiosity actually live longer than those whose curiosity has fallen by the wayside.

Perhaps the best thought with which to leave this subject is Rudyard Kipling's:

> I had six honest serving men,
> They taught me all I knew;
> Their names were Where and What and When
> And Why and How and Who.

It costs nothing and can do you no harm to utilize the services of these same six honest serving men.

Chapter 13

You Can Learn What You Really Want To

It is no great exaggeration to say that living is for the most part learning, and that the remainder of life is merely the carrying on in practice what has previously been learned. We begin to learn at least as soon as we begin to live; very probably the learning process commences some time before birth. It does not appear probable that we cease to learn until we are in the actual clutches of death.

KNIGHT DUNLAP

The above statement is true, of course. To learn is certainly of great importance to us as individuals or as members of society. Unfortunately, many of us reach a certain stage of learning, and go through the remainder of our lives coasting on the knowledge acquired till then.

Most of the things written in this book are geared toward enabling you to learn more — to pass that point. Curiosity, enthusiasm, interest, concentration, problem solving, memory and imagination, are all necessary ingredients for learning.

99

Curiosity is the starter; interest and enthusiasm are low gears; concentration and memory high gears; and accomplisnment is the smooth level ride.

We are all capable of learning, for the simple reason that none of us know it all — or ever will. I think that when we stop learning we begin to stagnate — to die. Everybody knows the cliché, "We learn something new every day." But do we? Can you honestly say that you learn something new every day?

Well, no matter. I'm not suggesting that you do. However, I am suggesting that there are probably many things you'd *like* to learn, but haven't yet — and probably don't ever really intend to.

Where to Begin — and How

This brings us to the crux of the matter. That is the difference between the wish to learn and the *will* to learn. How many times have you said to yourself, "I wish I could do that," or "I wish I had the abiltiy for this"?

Well, you can wish and wish but never really learn anything. It's the will to learn that does wonders. If you've gone through an art museum, or seen some good paintings anywhere, you may have said in an offhand manner, "Gee, I wish I understood, or knew, a little bit about art," and that was the end of it.

But if the will to learn is present, you can learn to understand art. I'm sure, if you look around, you'll find many places that teach art appreciation. If there is no such place near you, you can take a correspondence course. And these courses are not expensive; as a matter of fact, if you look hard enough, you'll find that you can even take some of them free of charge.

You may not become a connoisseur of art, but you *will* have a better understanding of it. And, according to William Allen White, "A little learning is *not* a dangerous thing to one who does not mistake it for a great deal."

The important thing here, as I've mentioned before, is to begin. Start learning a subject because you're interested in it, because you want to, and you'll continue to learn.

Do you want to learn how to play golf, or tennis; how to make a speech; write a story; be a better salesman; speak a foreign language or drive a car?

Fine! Stop wishing you could, and start to learn it. If you have the attitude, "Oh, I couldn't do that, I'm not smart enough," that's okay, too — as long as you don't allow it to stop you from trying.

Cicero once said, "The first step to knowledge is to know that we are ignorant."

If you thought you knew everything, you'd certainly never learn anything. Of course, some people who are the proud possessors of wealth feel that way. For those, I've always felt that our modern proverb, "If you're so smart, how come you're not rich?" should be changed to: "If you're so rich, how come you're not smart?"

Anyway, if you want to learn anything, *start!* I would suggest you start by looking over the entire field of the thing you want to learn. You want to learn to drive a golf ball? Try it once. Get the entire picture of the problem in your mind.

Then go to a good "pro" and have him lead you to your goal, step by step. The same holds true for anything you want to learn. The important thing, after you start is to set up a goal. Know just where you're heading. If you have only a vague idea of what you want to accomplish, your accomplishment *will* be vague at best.

Contrary to popular belief, repetition alone is not a particularly good way to learn anything. To repeat is to do things the same way; and when you first start learning anything, you're apt to make innumerable mistakes. Why repeat mistakes?

If your golf swing is wrong, repetition in this case will only help to ingrain your errors. The wrong method will form in your habit patterns, instead of the proper one.

If your sales approach is wrong, you can see a hundred customers a day, you may even make some sales, but the repetition of the wrong method is not making you a successful salesman.

Any golf or tennis pro will tell you that he would much rather teach a rank beginner than someone who has taught himself a little about the game. Before starting to teach, in the latter case, the pro first has to "unlearn" the pupil to rid him of his mistakes. These mistakes are difficult to get rid of, because they have become habitual through repetition.

So don't expect repeating something indefinitely to teach you to do it properly. If learning is to advance, you must eliminate errors as you progress. Set up challenges for yourself. This will help immensely. Try to watch others who are more proficient than you are. See what it is they do that you don't, or what they're doing differently.

I think that perhaps this is one of the best ways to learn anything. If you want to better your sales approach, watch a crack salesman work; If you want to learn public speaking, watch and listen to an established speaker in action.

And, most important, remember that these people were once learners too — fumbling, trying and eliminating errors. If they could do it, so can you!

When You Are Ready To Give Up

The bugaboo to look out for is discouragement. Allow yourself to become discouraged, or fed up, and you forfeit any progress you have made. Success or mastery of any new skill or subject is usually immediately around the corner of discouragement! It's just past that point, so why quit now?

You'll find that once you pass the lowest ebb of that "I give up" feeling, the light dawns, and another step in the right direction has been made.

I don't know why this is so, but it is. Perhaps it's because you are no longer pressing and tense when you're ready to give up. You're probably more relaxed then than at any other time during the learning process. And I'm sure you agree that it is much easier to learn when you're relaxed.

You'll also agree, I'm sure, that you drive a car perfectly when you are practicing with your instructor, but when you take the test for your driver's license, you tense up, and probably fail the first time.

When you're on the golf driving range, and nobody's around to see, you're relaxed and drive the ball straight as an arrow, two hundred yards. But once you're on the course with friends, you try too hard, tense up, try to send the ball too far, and usually wind up, topping, hooking, slicing — or missing it!

So you've a couple of things to keep in mind while in the process of trying to learn *anything*. First, try to relax. Second, don't allow yourself to become discouraged.

Remember that without mistakes there is no learning. Each mistake spotted and eliminated represents another step forward.

One error many people make is to learn something the wrong way and stick to it no matter what. Or they reach an impasse, and try to force their way past it, stubbornly — never admitting that they may be doing something wrong, and starting fresh.

Have you ever kept tropical fish? I have — and if you place a female Siamese Fighting Fish (Betta) in one tank, in sight of a male in another, the male will keep trying to reach her by crashing himself against the inside of his tank.

I've seen one male keep this up for almost an hour, without a sign of stopping, until I took the female away. This is stupid, of course — but fish *are* stupid.

Please don't allow yourself to fall into the trap of "persistence of error." If you can't get past a certain point in your learning, try a different approach. Try a few different approaches, as many as necessary, until you find the right one — or the right one for *you*.

This reminds me of the story of the gambler who was being cheated. A friend asked if he didn't realize that he couldn't win. The gambler answered, "Do you think I'm an idiot? Of course I know that he's cheating me. I just want to get even, then I'll quit."

According to some research material I've read, anyone can learn. There is an inborn capacity that makes the difference in *degrees* of learning. So far, nobody has been able to explain this inborn capacity — but why worry about it? Knowing that you can learn is the important thing. You'll never find out what your capacity is if you don't try to reach it — and I'm sure nobody ever does. Walter Dill Scott said, "It is more than probable that the average man could, with no injury to his health, increase his efficiency fifty per cent."

Some of us are more apt to learn mental skills than physical skills, and vice versa, of course. The examples I've used in this chapter apply to either. I also think that people should try to learn more in both areas. Too many of us, as I mentioned in the chaper on curiosity, go through life with blinkers on, never veering from our single path of least resistance.

Knowledge Is Power — Only If Put to Use

Don't be a spectator all your life — try to be a *doer* whenever possible. Ten times to one people are passive spectators instead of active participants. I believe this ratio should be reduced to at least four to one. You'll never learn anything new if you don't participate more often. Why don't you try it? The next time you're asked to participate or join in something new or different (for you), say "yes" instead of "no."

You'll learn more, that's for sure, and you'll open up new vistas for yourself. Even if you think you know something, use it; do it or you might just as well *not* know it. "Knowledge is power" only when it's put into action. If you don't use it, it remains potential power only.

Apropos of that, Jeremiah W. Jenks said, "The inlet of man's mind is what he learns; the outlet is what he accomplishes. If his mind is not fed by a continued supply of new ideas which he puts to work with purpose, and if there is no outlet in action, his mind becomes stagnant. Such a mind is a danger to the individual who owns it and is useless to the community."

Let's get back to the wish and the will to learn for a moment. The wish is necessary, of course, but as already mentioned, without the will there is little learning. For example, look at these nonsense syllables: brap, pim, mod, baf, nal, lin, rix, sul, pirn, dal, lig, fub.

Can you now, without looking at them again, remember them all? I doubt it. The fact is, you didn't pay much attention to them at all, did you? There was no wish *or* will to learn them. (Of course, if for any reason you had to remember nonsense syllables often, it would help you to read one of my books on memory training.) However, for our purposes right now, if you look at the syllables again, I'll wager you will remember most of them, for you are looking at them with a different attitude. You *would like* to remember them. That's the wish. If you really want to (have the will) you can remember them all in a short time.

The will to learn is the main ingredient for learning. Once you have that, proceed systematically, in an organized manner. Don't be slipshod about it, or your work will be many times as hard. Get a definite picture in your mind of what you want to learn, and you'll learn faster and better. A slipshod approach can only give you slipshod results.

Once you've got that picture in your mind of the thing you want to learn, take it step by step. Be sure you understand and can accomplish one step before continuing to the next. Once you've mastered all the steps, you can practice the thing you've learned as a whole.

The same holds true for mental skills, for learning or gathering information. If you want to learn a poem word for word, read it over a few times. Get the meaning, the beat, and feel of it. Then learn it a line or two at a time. Finally, practice reciting the entire poem.

Try to learn things preferably in the environment in which you intend to use them. I know that I never really learned to drive a car until I had battled the New York City traffic a number of times.

If you want to learn how to make a speech, make speeches. Get up in front of an audience whenever you can. You may do a terrible job at first, but you'll learn. Once you get the "feel" of anything you're trying to master, you're almost there. That "feel" will usually come, as I said before, when you're so discouraged you're about to give up.

Keep your goal in mind at all times. "Without motivation, learning is not apparent." Let your interest be your motivation.

For instance, boys learn baseball scores and records much more easily than their schoolwork — because they're generally more interested in baseball.

If, when you were studying a foreign language in school, you knew how important it might be to you, you would have learned that language faster and better than you did.

Many adults use the age-old excuse, "I'm too old to learn" or "You can't teach an old dog new tricks." Nonsense! All that is, is a good excuse! They don't really mean they're too old to learn. They mean they're too *lazy* to learn. Your *interest* may wane as you grow older, but not your ability to learn. E. L. Thorndike, an authority on adult education, said that, "Age is no handicap to learning a new trade, profession, or anything you want to do at any time of life."

So, when you feel you would like to learn something, turn that wish into a will to learn. Keep your interest sharp; follow the suggestions outlined here, and you shouldn't have too much difficulty.

And remember that, "Learning is wealth to the poor, an honor to the rich, an aid to the young, and a support and comfort to the aged" (John C. Lavatar).

Chapter 14

How to Improve Your Powers of Observation

It is the disease of not listening, the malady of not marking, that I am troubled withal.

SHAKESPEARE

Although I don't think it necessary or advisable for you to train your observation to the extent that Sherlock Holmes did, I do think that most of us could use a bit of sharpening up when it comes to observation.

Too many of us *see*, but rarely observe. Since the next two chapters pertain to memory, it is advisable to first discuss observation. The reason for this is that you can't very well remember anything if you haven't observed it. The eyes must see in order for the mind to interpret.

Do You Really See What You Look At?

For example, look at this box for a moment:

TREES
IN THE
THE
FOREST

x

Now what does it say? Does it say "Trees in the forest"? Look again; I'd like you to be sure before we continue.

All right. Have you checked it out? You can look at it again, if you like. If you still think it says, "Trees *in the* forest," then you're like most people: You're not observing. I've had people look at it ten times and swear that that's what it read. However, if you read it and point to each word as you do, you'll see that it reads, "Trees in *the the* forest"! There is an extra "the" in the phrase.

Perhaps you consider this example a bit sneaky. Well, I agree. Our minds tend to jump ahead, or to the end of familiar phrases. But I still think it proves that most of us just don't observe. Try this on your friends, and you'll concur.

Have you ever come out of a crowded theater or movie house at show break? Did you have to file out slowly because there were so many people trying to get out through one door? This has happened to me quite often. Then when I neared the door, I usually noticed two or three other exits nearby that nobody was using.

Nobody observed or saw those other doors. I'm inclined to think that they weren't observed because we usually do not see the obvious, the familiar or the commonplace.

If you don't agree with that, can you answer these questions? Do you know right now in which direction you turn the key to open your front door? Do you know which light is usually on top of the traffic signal, red or green? Do you know the exact balance in your checkbook? Do you know if the number six on your wristwatch is the Arabic 6 or the Roman numeral VI? Do you know which two letters of the alphabet are *not* on a dial telephone? Do you know which brand of cigarettes your best friend smokes? Do you know the color of the socks you're wearing right now?

I could go on and on with questions like these, but I don't think it's necessary. I imagine that everyone will agree that his or her capacity for observation can stand some improvement. The first thing you have to learn is to look at things with attention and awareness. The chapter on concentration, elsewhere in the book, goes into some detail on that.

If you want to practice — and observation becomes a habit with practice — you might try this: Get a piece of paper and try to list everthing in one of your rooms, without looking at the room, of course. List *everything* you can think of — pictures, furniture, ashtrays, everything.

Now go into the room and check. Notice all the things you didn't list, the things you never really observed. Try listing again. The list will get longer after each inspection of the room. Try the same thing with other rooms. Keep this up for a while, and your observation will improve outside as well as within your home.

Think of a familiar street, one that you've walked on many times. See if you can list all the stores on that street. Try listing them in their correct order. Then check yourself. If you didn't list all of them, try again. Then try it with other streets. Look in the window of one of those stores, then, without looking, see how many of the items you can list.

Try picturing a friend of yours and describing his or her face in minute detail. Then check the next time you see that person. Notice now what you never noticed before. There are many ways in which you can test your observation, and the more you test it, the better it will become. I'll leave you with that. I only want to assure you that if you look and listen with attention and awareness you'll not only save yourself a lot of time and trouble, but you'll improve your memory immediately. Samuel Johnson said, "The true art of memory is the art of attention."

A Bad Penny Turns Up!

While I'm on the subject of observation and memory, I don't want you to think that I forgot my promise to give you the solution to that "bad penny" problem.

You remember the predicament, don't you? You have twelve pennies, one of which is either lighter or heavier than the other eleven. You have a balancing scale upon which you're allowed only three weighings to tell which is the bad penny, and whether it's lighter or heavier.

I hope you've tried to work it out yourself, mainly because you'll understand this better if you have. At first the solution may sound more complicated than the problem. Take it step by step and you shouldn't have too much trouble. Three of the following paragraphs are lettered A, B, and C, because you are referred back to them once or twice. Now, here's the solution:

First of all, the way to begin is to weigh four against four. Let's take the simplest contingency first. You realize that one of two things can happen: either the scale balances or it doesn't. We'll assume now that it has balanced on your first weighing.

A. Of course, you know now that the bad penny is one of the four that you haven't weighed as yet. For the second weighing, weigh *three* of these four against three of the known good ones (any three of those you have already weighed). Again, either the scales will balance or they won't.

Assume again that they've balanced. Well, that's your second weighing, and you now know that the remaining penny, the one that hasn't been weighed at all, is the bad one. You have one weighing left. This one is used to find out if the penny is lighter or heavier. Simply weigh it against any one of the others. The scales cannot balance now. If the side of the remaining penny goes down, the penny is heavier than the other eleven; if it goes up, it's lighter.

That's one possible solution. But lets go back to the second weighing (Paragraph A), where you're balancing three including the possible bad one against three known good ones. What if the scales do *not* balance? Simple! Keep your eye on the side of the scale that has the probable bad one on it. If that side goes down while the other side goes up, then you know that one of those three is the bad one, and that it is heavier. If it goes up, then the bad penny is lighter.

B. Now, the third weighing: You are down to three possible bad pennies. Simply weigh one of them against another. If they balance, then the third (unweighed) one is the bad one. You already know whether it's lighter or heavier from the second weighing. If the scales don't balance, then knowing whether the bad penny is heavier or lighter, tells you which it is. If the second weighing told you that the penny was lighter, then the penny on the side of the scale which is now up, is the bad one. If you knew the bad penny was heavier, then the one which is down is the bad one!

Okay, there you have the complete solution *if* your first weighing balances. If the first weighing does not balance, it gets even more complicated. Go over this slowly, picturing it all in your mind as you do. At the end, I'll show you an easy way to try it, so that you can understand it more clearly.

If your first weighing is not balanced, the four pennies on the up side can be considered possible "lights," the four on the down side possible "heavies," while the four you haven't weighed are proved to be good ones.

The problem then breaks down to this: You must never leave more than three pennies for the last weighing. Here's how you do it. You are again, for the second weighing, going to weigh four against four, but with this difference — on the left (for description's sake) side of the scale, place one of the possible lights and three of the known good ones.

On the right side, place one possible heavy and three remaining possible lights. You will have one known good penny, and three possible heavies left over. Of course, you must keep track of which pennies are where.

C. Now again, the scales may balance or they may not. If they balance, you know that the bad penny is one of the three possible heavies that you did not weigh just now. So end as before (in Paragraph B): weigh one of the possible heavies against another. The one that goes down is the bad, heavier penny. If they should balance, the one remaining is the bad, heavier one.

However, what if the second weighing doesn't balance? Assume the left side goes up and the right side goes down. In this case, the bad penny must be either the one possible "light" on the left side, or the one possible "heavy" on the right. (You see why, don't you? It couldn't be one of the three possible lights on the right, or that side would have gone up. The other three on the left are already known good ones, so it couldn't be one of these.)

Okay, you're left with a possible heavy and a possible light for the last weighing. Simply weigh either one of them against a good one. If the possible heavy is the one you use, and it goes down, that's the bad penny. If they balance, then the possible light isn't "possible" any more — that's it.

Now, if the left side goes down and the right side goes up during the second weighing, the solution is a bit different. You would now know that the bad penny is one of the three possible lights on the right side. (It couldn't be the possible heavy or the right side would have gone down. It couldn't be the possible light on the left side, or that would have gone up.)

So you're left with three possible lights. End as in Paragraphs B and C. Weigh one of the lights against another. If one side goes up, that's your bad, lighter penny. If they balance, the remaining one is it.

That is the complete solution! I know it sounds awfully compli- cated, but it isn't really. Once you understand it, and learn to keep track of which penny is where, you'll know just how to handle it.

Here's an easy way to practice it. From a deck of cards take eleven black cards and one red card. The one red card will represent the bad penny. Now get a friend who's willing to help you and shuffle the twelve cards. Then place four of them face down, without look- ing at them, on your left and four on your right, as if you were putting them on a balancing scale. Have your friend decide, to him- self, whether the red card (bad penny) is to be heavier or lighter.

Now he looks at the cards, and indicates with his hands how the scale goes — which side is up and which is down or if they balance. You then continue along as per the above instructions. That's all. You'll see that after the third "weighing," you'll be able to tell him which is the red card, and whether it was heavier or lighter.

You may even want to go over the solution again, right now, using the card idea to help you follow it, and keep it clear in your mind. Have fun!

Here's one more thing for you to try. Read the following four lines. Count the "F's". Remember your total and check it against the correct answer which, if you keep reading, you'll find in a few pages. Don't look at the answer until you've read the four lines once or twice and arrived at a total number of F's, of course.

FINISHED FILES ARE THE RESULT
OF YEARS OF SCIENTIFIC STUDY
COMBINED WITH THE EXPERIENCE
OF MANY YEARS.

Chapter 15

How To Remember Anything — With the Least Effort

PATIENT: *Doctor, you've got to help me. I'm losing my memory, I'm sure. I hear a thing one moment, and forget it the next. I don't know what to do.*

DOCTOR: *When did you first notice this?*

PATIENT: *Notice what?*

I think that the one faculty that really exemplifies an organized mind is memory. Perhaps it's because this is closest to me that I feel it's most important. I wrote this, and the following chapter on remembering names and faces, over thirty years ago! I'm quite pleased and pleasantly surprised that, aside from a bit of editing, it all holds up quite well. Obviously, I'm only scratching the surface.

Anyone can learn to improve his or her memory. All we wish to remember must be associated in some way with something we *already* remember. Anything you remember now, you are associating in this way.

113

How many times have you seen or heard something which made you snap your fingers and exclaim, "Oh, that reminds me!"? The thing that reminded you may have had no obvious connection with the thing it reminded you of. Yet there was an association there someplace. The trouble is that such associations are made subconsciously. If you can learn to make them *consciously*, you will have a trained memory.

Conscious associations have been used for years to help people remember almost anything. The sentence, "*E* very *G* ood *B* oy *D* oes *F* ine," helped you remember the lines of the staff or treble clef when you went to school. The phrase, "Never be*lie* ve a *lie*," helped you remember that "i" comes before "e" in spelling "believe." The word "homes" helps to recall the names of the Great Lakes: *H* uron, *O* ntario, *M* ichigan, *E* rie and *S* uperior.

The Secret of Memory Association

I don't intend to go into a complete memory training course in this book; but I do want to show you how systemization and organization can help you to remember in a way that you've never remembered before.

For example, look at these twelve words: book, flower, cigarette, eyeglasses, shoe, suitcase, car, clock, baseball, pen, necktie, ship.

Now, do you think you could remember all these words in that order, from first to last, after seeing or hearing them only once? I doubt it. I've yet to find anyone with an untrained memory who could do it. Well, I think I can teach you now, in this chapter, how to memorize these twelve (or any twelve, or more) objects, in order, forward *and* backward.

I've already told you that it's done via association. This simply means that you must connect or tie up two objects at a time — and to make the association stronger, they must be tied up in a ridiculous or illogical manner. We always tend to remember ridiculous, ludicrous and violent things rather than pleasant ones.

Okay, the first object is "book," the next is "flower." Now you must make a picture in your mind of some sort of ridiculous association between these two. For example, you might "see" a flower reading a book — or books growing in a garden instead of flowers. Pick an association that you feel is most ridiculous, and see it in your mind's eye for just a second.

If you don't actually *see* the picture, you won't remember the objects. Once you've seen it, forget it and go on to the next one.

"Cigarette" is the object we want to remember now. Associate that with "flower." You're smoking a flower, or a flower is smoking a cigarette, or cigarettes (lit) are growing instead of flowers. Pick one, and picture it for a moment.

Eyeglasses. See a large cigarette wearing eyeglasses, or you're smoking a pair of eyeglasses; or you have two cigarettes over your eyes instead of glasses.

Have you got the idea? You always associate the present object with the preceding one, and in so doing, you form a chain which should lead from one object to the next. Each association must be illogical and it *must be seen in the mind's eye.*

Here are some suggestions for ridiculous associations for the rest of the items. In each case, select the one you feel is most ridiculous and take a second to picture it.

Eyeglasses to shoe. You're wearing eyeglasses on your feet instead of shoes (the lens break and cut your feet). Or a gigantic shoe is wearing glasses. (See the picture.)

Shoes to suitcase: You're wearing suitcases instead of shoes. Or you open a suitcase and a million shoes fly out and kick you in the face. (See your association.)

Suitcase to car: You're driving a large suitcase instead of a car. Or you're carrying a car instead of a suitcase. Or a car is carrying a suitcase. Or a suitcase is driving a car. (Pick one and see it.)

Car to clock: You're driving a gigantic clock instead of a car. Or a large car is on your table and you look at it to tell time. Or a large clock is your chauffeur and is driving the car. (Be sure to see the picture.)

Clock to baseball: You're hitting a clock instead of a baseball. Or a large clock (or team of clocks) is playing baseball. (Be sure to see the picture.)

Baseball to pen: You're hitting the ball with a pen. Or you're writing with a baseball instead of a pen. Or a large pen is playing baseball. (Don't just see the words, see the actual picture.)

Pen to necktie: You're wearing a pen instead of a necktie. Or a large pen is wearing a necktie. Or you're writing on your tie with a pen. (See the picture.)

Necktie to ship: You're wearing a ship instead of a necktie. Or you're sailing on a gigantic tie instead of a ship. Or a million ties (instead of people) are sailing on a ship. (Select one and see the picture.)

All right: if you've "seen" each one of these pictures in your mind's eye, you should be able to start with "book," and memorize right down to "ship"! Try it.

When you think of "book" the picture of the flower reading it will come to mind. Then the thought of "flower" will make you think of smoking one instead of a "cigarette." Then you're wearing cigarettes instead of "eyeglasses." Continue down to "ship."

You can go even further. If you've made the associations ridiculous and strong enough, you should be able to start with "ship" and remember back right up to "book." Try it and amaze yourself.

This particular idea can be used to remember anything in sequence. I've mentioned in the chapter on public speaking that the best way to deliver a speech is to try to know it thought for thought. Well, that's a sequence.

If you've got your speech written out, go through it and take one *key* word from each thought. Your key word must be one that will bring the entire thought to mind. Then simply "link" all these words just as you did with the above objects, and you can throw away your notes!

If you go over your "link" a few times, you'll find that it's easier to remember than to forget them. Try remembering the twelve objects tomorrow, and you'll see that you still can.

As you deliver or finish one thought during your speech, the next one will come to mind almost automatically. And so on, to your conclusion.

How to Remember Things in Any Order

When it comes to remembering things in and out of order, or by number — well, as I said, I don't want to go into a complete memory course here. My books on the subject teach the complete "peg" system for remembering numbers of any length. However, just to illustrate the power of an organized mind plus a little imagination, let me teach you a way, a limited way, to memorize, say, sixteen items, in and out of order. It will also be handy for remembering your daily errands, shopping lists, appointments, and many other things.

Keep in mind that anything you wish to remember must be associated with something you *already* remember. I'll give you sixteen things to memorize once, and that will help you to remember sixteen other things any time you like.

Of course, you could memorize any list of objects as a "peg" list. However, the following one is so simple because each object is selected to represent a number for a definite reason, and it can represent only one number. You won't have to count through the entire list to figure out which number is represented by the object.

For No. 1, picture a magician's *wand*. A wand standing upright looks like the numeral 1. (Illustrations.)

For No. 2, picture a swan. With a little stretch of the imagination, a *swan* looks like the figure 2. (Illustrations.)

For No. 3, I usually picture a three-leaf *clover*.

For No. 4, you can picture anything with four legs — a *table*, a *chair* or a *four-legged animal*. (Illustrations.)

For No. 5, picture a five-pointed *star*. (Illustrations.)

For No. 6, picture an elephant's *trunk*, curved to look like a 6. (Illustrations.)

For No. 7, a *flag* waving in the breeze. (Illustrations.)

For No. 8, picture an *hourglass*. (Illustrations.)

For No. 9, a man's *pipe* standing on its stem. (Illustrations.)

For No. 10, picture a *bat and ball*. The bat represents the digit 1, and the ball represents the zero. (Illustrations.)

For No. 11, my original picture was of two strands of *spaghetti*. (Illustrations.) So spaghetti will always represent No. 11 for me.

For No. 12, see a picture of a *clock* stopped at 12:00 o'clock. (Illustrations.)

For No. 13, you can picture either a black cat, or someone walking under a *ladder*. (Illustrations.)

For No 14, picture a bolt of *lightning* shaped like 14. (Illustrations.)

For No. 15, I originally pictured myself stepping into an *elevator* and saying "fifteenth floor, please." So picture an elevator for this number. (Illustrations.)

For No. 16, picture a *road sign* that says, "Route 16." (Illustrations.)

With the little "memory aid" that I've given you for each object, you should have no trouble remembering them easily. Practice until you know them in and out of order. Here's the list once more.

1. wand
2. swan
3. clover
4. table
5. star
6. elephant's trunk
7. flag
8. hourglass
9. pipe
10. bat and/or ball
11. spaghetti
12. clock
13. ladder (black cat)
14. lightning
15. elevator
16. sign

Using the Memory Key

Now, if you have these in your mind, I'll show you how to use them. Don't try this until you're sure you know the sixteen "peg" words thoroughly. Let's say you want to do this as a stunt, to show off for your friends. Have someone call the numbers haphazardly, and give you any object for each number. He's to write them as he calls them, so that he'll remember them.

When all sixteen are filled in, you will be able to remember all the items in order, or he can call any number and you will tell him the item, or he can call the item and you will tell him its numerical position!

Here's all you have to do: When an object is called, simply associate it in a ridiculous manner to the "peg" that represents the number called. For example, if "window" is called for No. 9, see a *pipe* smashing a window, or a window smoking a pipe.

Why don't you try it now? I'll give you the sixteen items haphazardly, with a suggestion on how to associate each one. Make all the associations as ridiculous as you can; see them in your mind's eye, and you'll surprise yourself.

No. 9: window — I've already helped you with this one.

No. 16: wallet — see a large wallet instead of a road sign, or you open your wallet and a large sign falls out.

No. 3: bird cage — see a clover instead of a bird locked in a bird cage.

No. 11: ashtray — see yourself dropping ashes into your spaghetti.

No. 7: newspaper — you're waving a newspaper instead of a flag, or you're reading a flag.

No. 14: radio — a large bolt of lightning demolishes your radio, or you turn on the radio and lightning shoots out of it.

No. 1: hat — you're waving a hat instead of a wand, or you wave your wand at a hat and it disappears, or you're wearing a wand for a hat.

No.12: waste paper basket — see a basket on your mantel instead of a clock, or the basket is filled with many clocks.

No. 5: bed — see a large star sleeping in a bed, or a bed hangs in the sky instead of a star.

No. 15: light bulb — see yourself going up in a bulb instead of an elevator, or an elevator door opens and a million light bulbs roll out.

No. 6: typewriter — see an elephant typing with his trunk, or an elephant has a typewriter in place of a trunk.

No. 13: telephone — see a telephone climbing a ladder, or you're talking into a ladder instead of a phone, or a ladder is talking on the phone.

No. 4: gun — see yourself using a large gun for a table, or a table is shooting a gun.

No. 10: house — see a house playing baseball, or you're wrecking a house with a baseball bat.

No. 2: briefcase — see a briefcase floating on a lake like a swan, or you open your briefcase and a swan swims out.

No. 8: picture — see an hourglass framed on your wall instead of a picture, or you keep turning your picture upside down to allow the sand to shift, as in an hourglass.

Now you should be able to call off all these items from 1 to 16. Think of your "peg" for No. 1. That's a magician's wand. You recall that you were wearing a wand instead of a *hat*. Therefore, No. 1 is hat. Your "peg" for No. 2 is swan. A *briefcase* was floating on a lake instead of a swan. No. 3's "peg" is clover — a three-leaf clover is in a *birdcage*. The "peg" for No. 4 is table — and a table was shooting a *gun,* and so on.

See if you can fill in all the blanks:

1.	_____	9.	_____
2.	_____	10.	_____
3.	_____	11.	_____
4.	_____	12.	_____
5.	_____	13.	_____
6.	_____	14.	_____
7.	_____	15.	_____
8.	_____	16.	_____

Did you get most of them? If you missed one or two, your associations weren't strong enough. Strengthen them now. Of course, if an object is called you can give the *number* immediately. Say "telephone" is called. Do you recall your picture of talking into a ladder instead of a phone? Ladder is the "peg" for No. 13 — therefore "telephone" must be No. 13.

Well, I hope I've shown you how a bit of organization and imagination can enable you to do something you've never been able to do before. I admit that this idea is limited, although you could make the list longer if you wanted to. However, the phonetic sound "peg" system taught in my other books and at my seminars can be brought into the thousands without any trouble at all.

Still, the system explained here can be used for a variety of purposes. If you have a list of errands and appointments to remember, simply tie them up with the "peg" list. You have to have your car washed — associate car with wand. Then you have a dental appointment — so associate dentist with swan. You have to buy an umbrella, associate umbrella with clover. You've got a bill to pay, associate bill with table, and so on with all your errands for the day.

Once you've compiled the list, simply go through it, one "peg" word at a time, to remember what you've got to do next. If you've got a sales talk to memorize, you can associate a different point with each "peg" word. I'm sure you'll find many ways of using the list.

Now that you see how your memory can be improved, you should be pleased to know that the following chapter will teach you how to remember names and faces.

Here's the answer to the "F" question asked at the end of the preceding chapter. There are *six* F's in the 4-line sentence. Ninety-nine percent of those who try it count three F's. Most eyes miss the F in "of" — and there are three of those. Even if you came up with the correct answer (6), try it on friends; you'll be amazed at how many see only three F's. You can type the four lines onto an index card, exactly as shown, so that you can carry it with you.

Chapter 16

How To Remember Names and Faces

Memory, the daughter of attention, is the teeming mother of knowledge.

MARTIN TUPPER

At my lectures and performances I remember the names and faces of everybody in the audience! Perhaps you saw me do just that recently on the Jack Paar Show. (That's a giveaway, isn't it?! Since writing this, I've been on just about every national television show here and abroad — twenty-three times with Johnny Carson, at last count.) I've remembered as many as seven hundred people in one evening, after meeting them only once! I mention this, not to brag, but to try to prove to you that it can be done.

A universal complaint nowadays is: "I can't remember **names.**" No problem with the faces, of course; it's always the name that creates the problem. I've never heard anyone say, "I remember your name, but I simply can't remember your face!"

Well, the reason for this is quite simple. We all tend to remember the things we see much better than the things we hear. We always see the face, but usually only hear the name — therein lies the problem.

123

There have been many systems devised to help people remember names. One man always asked people whose name he couldn't recall whether it was spelled with an "e" or an "i." This was fine, until he asked the question of a Mrs. Betch!

No, I'm afraid this won't do. The best, and as far as I'm concerned the only, way to remember names is to tie the name to the person's face. As long as you usually "place the face" anyway, why not take advantage of that, and let the face bring the name to mind for you? As a matter of fact, the system of association that I'm about to describe for you will work both ways. The face will bring the name to mind; and the name will help you to picture the face.

Remembering Names Without Faces

However, before going into the system itself, I think I can considerably improve your memory for names without it.

Many people who constantly complain that they forget names don't really forget them — they never remember them in the first place. As a matter of fact, sometimes they never even hear them.

Think of that for a moment! Many times, you never even *hear* the name, so how in the world can you remember *or* forget it? The first rule for remembering names is: be sure you hear the name when you're introduced to someone!

People are flattered if you show interest in their names, so you needn't be afraid to ask someone to repeat a name if you don't think you've heard it properly. The people who have reputations for prodigious memories for names won those reputations via the expedient of one little sentence: "I'm sorry, but I didn't get your name!"

Once you've made sure you've heard the name — if it's a familiar one, or if it's similar to that of a friend or relative, or one that you've never heard before — mention it. As I said, people will love you when you make a fuss over their names, and one or two remarks about it will help to drive it into your memory.

Now, if you simply make it a point to *use* the name occasionally during the conversation, you'll be amazed at how you'll improve your memory. I don't mean to keep repeating it like an idiot, but do use it occasionally, and particularly when you say, "Good night" or "Good-bye."

If you follow these simple rules, all you're really doing is concentrating on the name in a way you've never done before. Now this will take care of about — oh, 25 per cent of the problem. If you're interested in solving the remaining 75 per cent, read on.

As I mentioned, the best way to remember names and faces is to associate the name to the face. The method is really easy. There are two steps involved. The first one is to make the name *mean* something; so let's discuss that for a moment. Actually, there are three categories that names fall into: (1) names that already mean something; (2) names that may have no meaning, but remind you of something tangible; and (3) names that have no meaning at all.

Of course, you have the least problem with names that already mean something, or that remind you of something. The problem is the meaningless names. Let me give you a few examples of each type, and then I'll show you what to do about the third category. Names like Brown, Stern, Taylor, Green, Coyne, Carpenter, Sommer, Byrd, Butler, Locke already have meaning.

Dempsey, Sullivan, McCarthy, Fitch, Arcaro and names of that type may have no particular meaning to you, but should remind you of something, bring a certain picture to mind. Sullivan and Dempsey should make you think of fighters. McCarthy might make you think of a ventriloquist's dummy (Charlie McCarthy). Fitch is the brand name of a shampoo; Arcaro should make you picture a jockey.

The list of names that have no meaning is a long one. You hear them every day. Names like Krakauer, Karowski, Cortell, Kolodny, Cohen, Platinger, Smolenski, Gordon, and so on ad infinitum.

The system I call "substitute words or thoughts" is what enables you to picture *any* name. All you have to do is make up a word or phrase that sounds as close as possible to the name you wish to remember, and that has some meaning to you.

For example: the name Steinwurtzel would probably confuse you ordinarily. But if you picture a beer *stein* that's covered with gold to make it *worth selling* — "stein worth sell" would help you think of Steinwurtzel!

There is no name — I repeat, no name — that cannot be broken down in some way in order to make it meaningful or tangible to you. I don't care how silly or ridiculous your substitute word or phrase is — as a matter of fact, usually, the sillier the better.

For a name like Krakauer, you could picture either a cracked clock — "crack hour" — or a "cracked cow," which is close enough. For Platinger, picture a plate that's been injured — "plate injure" — Platinger. A *small* camera (*lens*) *ski*ing, would bring to mind Smolenski.

For a name like Gordon, I always picture a garden. You see, after a bit of practice you'll start using certain pictures for certain names all the time. For instance, I always picture an ice cream *cone* for Cohen, or a black*smith*'s hammer for Smith.

Incidentally, it isn't necessary to get the *entire* sound of the name into your substitute word or phrase. *Remember the main element, and the incidentals will fall into place.* This system is merely an aid to your true memory. If the name you want to memorize is Belden, the picture of a bell would suffice; your true memory would take care of the rest of it. Of course, a bell in a den would make it definite.

The important thing is that in order to find a substitute word for a name you *must* hear it in the first place. Then you automatically become interested in the name, and interest is essential to memory.

Okay, I think by now you've got the idea — so long as you realize that *any* name can be made to mean something. As a sort of extreme example, I once had to remember the name Pukczyva. It is pronounced "Puck-shiv-va." I pictured a hockey puck shivering with cold. Recently I met a Mr. Bentavagnia. It is pronounced "bent-a-vay-nya." I pictured someone *bend*ing a weather *vane*.

Many names have similar endings, like "ly," "ton," "berg," etc. Make up a word for each of these and use it consistently. A *lea* is a meadow; a barbell, dumbell or any weight can be used to represent *ton*; and *berg* means mountain in German, or visualize an iceberg.

As far as prefixes are concerned — well, for any name beginning with "Mc" or "Mac," picture a Mack truck; for "Stein," a beer stein; and for "Berg", an iceberg or mountain. For Mr. Macatee, I'd picture a Mack truck running over a cup of tea: "Mack tea" — Macatee. For the name Steinberg, you might see a beer *stein* on top of an ice*berg*.

By the way, all this is a very individual thing. The first thought that comes to me upon hearing a name may differ from the one that comes to you. That's as it should be — but usually the first thing that comes to mind is the one to use.

Before going on to show you how to associate a name to a face, perhaps you'd like a bit of practice. Well, why don't you see what you can do with the following names? I'll give you my suggestions afterward, but first see what you can do on your own.

Stapleton	Zimmerman
Brady	Kolodny
Welling	Citron
Jordan	Zauber
Schwartzberg	Robinson
Fishter	McGarrity
Cortell	Kusek

Carruthers

Here are my first thoughts on each of them:

Stapleton — See so many staples that they weigh a ton; or you're stapling a barbell (or whatever you're using to represent ton). "Staple ton" — Stapleton.

Brady — You can picture a girl's braid, or you're braiding the lines of a gigantic letter "E." "Braid E" — Brady.

Welling — See a well filled with ink instead of water. "Well ink" — Welling.

Jordan — Picture a river, the River Jordan. Or a jaw falling down. "Jaw down" — Jordan.

Schwartzberg — See an iceberg covered with warts. "Warts berg" — Schwartzberg.

Fishter — See yourself fishing and catching a toe or you're tearing a fish. "Fish toe," "fish tear" — Fishter.

Cortell — A length of cord is gossiping or telling. "Cord tell" — Cortell.

Zimmerman — Picture a man cooking or simmering in a large pot. "Simmer man" — Zimmerman.

Kolodny — See a knee that's all different colors. "Colored knee" — Kolodny.

Citron — Picture someone sitting and running at the same time. (A citrus fruit would do it too.) "Sit run" — Citron.

Zauber — See yourself sawing a bear in half, or sawing in the nude. "Saw bear," "Saw bare" — Zauber.

Robinson — See a robin and its son; or you're robbing your own son. "Robin son," "robbing son" — Robinson.

McGarrity — A Mack truck is carrying thousands of cups of tea. "Mack carry tea" — McGarrity.

Kusek — See a cue stick being sick. "Cue sick" — Kusek.

Carruthers — See a car with udders (like a cow). "Car udders" — Carruthers.

Putting the Right Name to the Right Face

Well, that's the first step — making the name meaningful. Now for step number two, which is tying the name, or the substitute word for it, to the face. All you have to do is look at the face and pick out one outstanding feature. This can be anything — high forehead, low forehead, large nose, big ears, lines, clefts, thick lips, thin lips, close-set eyes, dimples, large chin, receding chin — anything.

Again, this is an individual thing. Two people may look at the same face and pick two different features. But the one that's outstanding to you now is the one that will be outstanding when you see that face again. More important, while looking for that outstanding feature, you are getting a picture of the entire face in your mind, automatically.

When you've decided on the outstanding feature, associate the substitute word for the name to that feature in some ridiculous way. That's all there is to it!

Make your associations in the same manner that you learned to do with objects — make them ridiculous and "see" them in your mind's eye. If you meet a Mr. Markel who has great bushy eyebrows, you might see yourself marking those eyebrows with large letter "L's." "Mark L" — Markel. See that picture in your mind as you look at the person's face, and the odds are that when you see that face again, the eyebrows will make you think of the name.

Keep in mind, please, that all this is really a means to an end. Once a name is fixed indelibly in your memory, you can forget your associations. Also, what this system is really doing is forcing you to be interested in, listen to and concentrate on the name — and be interested in, look at and concentrate on the face. If you could do this all the time without the system, you wouldn't *need* the system.

The use of the system, however, makes it easier to do, since we're all basically lazy, and don't want to concentrate. Before you know it, the system will become habit, and you'll do it almost automatically — that is, if you start using it now.

A few more examples:

Mr. Galloway has a deep cleft in his chin. Picture a girl or *gal* going *away*, or falling *away*, out of that cleft.

Mr. Sachs has a high forehead. See that forehead *as* a large *sack;* or thousands of sacks are flying out of his forehead.

Mr. Van Nuys has bulging eyes. See two large *vans* making lots of *noise* driving out of those eyes.

Mr. Smith has a large nose. See that nose as a black*smith*'s hammer; or you're hammering on his nose with the hammer.

Of course, the best way to practice all this is to go ahead and do it. The next time you're introduced to a few people at a time, try the system — you'll be amazed, I assure you. Don't feel that it takes too long to do it, either. After a minimum of practice you'll have found a substitute word for the name (if necessary) and associated it to an outstanding feature of the face in about as much time as it takes to say, "Hello."

If you like, you can use a magazine or newspaper for practice. Cut out pictures of faces and use them as practice cards. Either make up names or use their real ones, and apply the system. Even though a picture is a one-dimensional thing, it will still prove the system's effectiveness.

Well, that about does it. There is much more I could teach you about memory, but I won't here. I just wanted to prove how organizing your mind, and a bit of imagination and concentration thrown in, could and must improve your memory.

Chapter 17

How to Make Anyone Like You — The Secret of Personality

We possess by nature the factors out of which personality can be made, and to organize them into effective personal life is every man's primary responsibility.

HARRY EMERSON FOSDICK

The other day I was talking to a friend who mentioned that he'd watched a television star the night before. "He's just great!" was his opinion. I asked him if this star could dance? The answer was no. Could he sing? No. Was he a comedian? Not really. Well, why was he so wonderful? "Oh, he's such a nice guy!"

I guess this is of great importance to all of us: to possess the talent of making people like us — more so in everyday life than in television, I'm sure. Macauley once said that "popularity is power," and to be popular among your own friends and acquaintances, it goes without saying that they must like you.

The way you look, the way you act and the way you talk are the three things that "set" your personality. The way you think is what

131

controls your looks, actions and words. It is not an easy task for me to teach you how to obtain a good personality; I can only give you some general hints on how to make others like you.

You Must Like Others First

The best way, of course, is to be interested in other peoples' interests. There is no better way to gain their attention and their interest. I know of one man who makes his living interviewing celebrities for his newspaper. His specialty is in getting somewhere with people who usually don't like to talk to reporters. His secret is a simple one. Before an interview, he makes it his business to take the time to find out what the interviewee is interested in.

He studies up on some of these things, so that he can show an intelligent curiosity and interest in them. It's surprising how those that ordinarily "clam up" will talk to him. And you can do worse than to utilize this idea when talking to anyone.

Everybody looks for and desires approval — to be liked and appreciated by others. And those who act as if they don't want, or don't care for, appproval desire it most of all. They are, perhaps, too wrapped up in themselves — which, incidentally, makes a small package. It seems impossible to me that one can be interested only in one's self and be popular at the same time. Charles H. Parkhurst said it this way: "The man who lives by himself and for himself is apt to be corrupted by the company he keeps."

I personally have started many lasting friendships by showing interest (even if it's feigned interest at first) in the projects, troubles, ambitions and general interests of others.

You've got to learn to like people in order to make them like you. Try using the system of "similar attitudes." Most people will act toward you as you act toward them. It's easy enough to prove this statement. Frown at the next person you talk to, and the odds are he'll frown right back at you. Act as if you're looking into a mirror when you converse with friends or acquaintances. Keep that in mind, because your acquaintance's attitudes are usually reflections of your own actions.

I know a few cynics who think the world, or rather the people in it, are in bad shape. Nobody cares about these people, so they don't care about anyone. Of course, they're lonely people — they insist on building barricades around themselves, instead of bridges. You can build bridges by learning to smile instead of frown.

We've all heard that it takes more muscles to frown than it does to smile. I don't know if that's true, but why not act as if it were. Make it easy on yourself — smile!

To Win Friends — Be One

If you're lonely, if you don't have enough friends — well, *be* a friend and you'll have friends. Go out of your way occasionally to help someone, as you would want a friend to help you. Remember this quote by G. Bailey: "It is one of the beautiful compensations of life that no man can sincerely try to help another, without helping himself," or James Barrie's: "Those who bring sunshine to the lives of others cannot keep it from themselves." Remember them and *live* by them — you'll be a happier and better person for it.

Don't complain about people not being kind if you're not kind yourself. I believe that every kindness you show will come back to you someday, some way — if not from the people you showed it to — well then, from others. Sooner or later everything balances out. Bread cast upon the waters, you know.

Walter S. Landor said that "Kindness in ourselves is the honey that blunts the sting of unkindness in another." Most people are trying to solve the same problems, the same war of nerves, the same hard fight that you are. Keep that in mind the next time you're about to be unkind to someone. De Grellet wrote: "I shall pass through this world but once. If, therefore, there is any kindness I can show, or any good thing I can do, let me do it now; let me not defer it or neglect it, for I shall not pass this way again."

I don't hold with actions or attitudes that people display for which apologies are necessary but aren't always given. I refer to those people who excuse their unkindness or impoliteness with "I was very busy" or "I didn't feel well" or "I was in a bad mood."

I was in a hospital visiting a friend who had suffered a heart attack. He wanted to make an important phone call. He held his private telephone off the hook for about four or five minutes and got no response. Thinking that the switchboard operator couldn't hear the buzz, or that there might be something wrong with the phone itself, he clicked the receiver a few times.

Suddenly he heard the operator's sharp voice: "What the h___ are you clicking about? I'll give you a line when I'm good and ready!" The patient was stunned and complained bitterly. I went to a public booth to make the call for him. Some time later, the manager of the hospital came into the room and told my friend that the operator had been very busy at the time.

Well now, that's just what I'm talking about. It certainly would seem that a man who had just suffered a heart attack, and was in the hospital because of it, deserved a little more courtesy, even if the telephone operator was three times as busy. And it would have taken less time to say something like "I'm awfully sorry, but I'll give you a line the moment one is free" than it did for her original discourteous remark. I can only assume that that operator is a terribly unhappy person.

There is *always* time for courtesy! Stop using your sickness, pains, worries and troubles as excuses for avoiding it. Remember the next time you snap at someone because you've got a stomach ache that he may be dying, for all you know. Justice Felix Frankfurter said that, "Courtesy is the lubricant of society," and I couldn't agree more wholeheartedly.

Just as you like to be appreciated, show others your appreciation. The two most beautiful words we can utter are not used often enough nowadays. They are: "Thank you." Use them more often and you'll hear them more often.

So you may think the world's against you. You may want to change everything and everybody — but, believe me, you'll find that the best way, in many instances, to change your friends, acquaintances, husband or wife is to change yourself. And, according to Thomas à Kempis: "Be not angry that you cannot make others as you wish them to be, since you cannot make yourself (entirely) as you wish to be."

We Are All Funnier Than We Think

I think that the most essential ingredient for a good personality is a sense of humor. Learn to laugh a little more at yourself and at life. Sooner or later, you're going to laugh at the petty annoyances and frustrations that face you now; why not laugh at them now, to begin with? And, incidentally, a sense of humor does not mean laughing at something happening to somebody else that would make you angry if it happened to *you*!

I don't know of a better antidote for nervousness or tenseness than a sense of humor. The problem, of course, is that those who do not possess this valuable attribute don't know it. According to Frank M. Colby "Men will confess to treason, murder, arson, false teeth, or a wig. How many of them will own up to a lack of humor?"

Well, I don't know that it's a question of "owning up" to it; it's rather a question of *knowing* that you suffer from a lack of humor.

Look into it; check yourself. Ask yourself if you're not taking yourself much too seriously. The heaviest burden you can carry is that proverbial chip on your shoulder. Shake it loose via a sense of humor. As with everything else discussed in this book, it's all in the mind. Try to think a little less about what's happening to you, and a bit more about what you *cause* to happen, and you'll see more clearly the humor in most things.

Harry Emerson Fosdick said, "Reduce to a minimum the things that mortify you. To be ugly, to lack desired ability, to be economically restricted — such things are limitations, but if they become humiliations it is because inwardly you make them so." Limitations, you see, can be overcome or compensated for, but humiliations — well, they can set up insurmountable barriers.

Your sense of humor will stop these barriers from becoming higher or wider. You've got to look at certain things with the proverbial grain of salt. Shrug, and carry on anyway. The limerick that follows, written by Anthony Euwer, and often quoted by President Woodrow Wilson, points out just the attitude I have in mind:

> As a beauty I'm not a great star.
> Others are handsomer far;
> But my face — I don't mind it
> Because I'm behind it;
> It's the folks out in front that I jar.

Do You Talk Too Much — or Too Little?

Now, the one thing all normal people possess is the ability to talk. And it's mainly by the way you talk that others judge your personality. I'm not referring to your diction, grammar, and tone, although these things are important. No; I mean, essentially, *what* you say. Robert Louis Stevenson wrote: "To talk is our chief business in this world; and talk is by far the most accessible of pleasures. It costs nothing in money; it is all profit; it completes our education, founds and fosters our friendships, and can be enjoyed at any age and in almost every state of health."

This is all true, but there is another saying that goes: "The thing most frequently opened by mistake is the human mouth." I think most of us — except professional critics, of course — would be much better off if we followed this advice: if you can't say something complimentary or favorable, keep your mouth shut and say nothing!

Quite often criticism only manages to throw a bad light on the critic. It's also easier to criticize than to be right or to help — so most of us do it. You'll improve your personality immediately if you stop it.

Another method for improving your personality fast is to stop talking about your favorite subject — *you* — so much. Talk about the other person *to* that other person, and he or she will love you for it. Montaigne put it in a nutshell: "When all is summed up, a man never speaks of himself without loss; his accusations of himself are always believed; his praises never."

Are you afraid to talk to people? Are you the type who looks at the floor, or over the other fellow's head, or at his right ear while you're conversing? The best place to look when talking to someone (unless you're on the phone) is squarely into his eyes. I know one man who practiced looking into his own eyes, in a mirror, for half and hour at a time. He was then able to look into the eyes of others while talking to them.

I don't mean that it's necessary to get so close that you breathe into peoples' faces. If you glare at them too hard, you will surely make your listeners uncomfortable.

Learn, also, to listen attentively (even if you've heard it before) again looking into the speaker's eyes. Listen well, and you'll be given credit for speaking well. And if you're a good listener, you *will* talk better.

Don't be afraid to talk. Erasmus said that by speaking men learn to speak. Just try to take a middle ground and give the other guy a chance, too. The worst thing you can ever do is to appear bored when someone is talking to you. Remember this: you're never really bored with others — or anything, for that matter — you are bored only with yourself.

Some other important points: Don't always insist on being so darn truthful. I'd prefer it if people thought more about being kind than being painfully truthful. William Blake put it this way: "A truth that's told with bad intent, beats all the lies you can invent." Malicious gossip, even if it's true, will not enhance your personality.

Use judgment and discretion; there are times when the exact truth is unnecessary. I once received a strange introduction at a lecture. The speaker originally booked had been taken ill, and he asked me to fill in for him at the last minute. The program chairman said something to this effect: "Ladies and gentlemen, I'm sorry to have to tell you that Mr. _____ has been taken ill. So, unfortunately, instead of Mr. _____, may I present Mr. Harry

Lorayne." (This occurred three decades ago; I don't "fill in" anymore!)

Of course, he didn't mean it the way it sounded (at least I hope not), but it would have been better if he had simply introduced me. There is no need to be utterly frank at such a time.

A perennial bore, of course, is the life-of-the-party type who just *isn't* the life-of-the-party type. Here again, it's important to learn to "know thyself." There are people who evoke screams of delight when they parade around with lampshades on their heads; others get yawns or looks of annoyance. Be sure you're not the latter type before you start cutting up.

It is the easiest thing in the world to advise another; the most difficult not to do it. Even when friends ask for your advice, they usually want you to tell them exactly what they've already made up their minds to do. If you feel you must give advice, tell people to do what they want to do, or don't give it. I guess advice is the only commodity that's more blessed to receive than to give.

And don't be afraid to say, "I don't know." I've never been able to understand people who give directions when they're not really sure themselves. For some reason, people are ashamed to admit that they don't know the way to Main Street or Broadway. Many's the time I've asked for directions and been sent on a wild goose chase. So, remember — if you don't know, say so.

Another reason why some folks are disliked is that they enjoy ordering people around. Preface your requests with phrases like, "I'd appreciate it if. . ." or "How do *you* think this should be done?" and you should have no trouble in this area. Of course, the best way to get anyone to do anything is to find a way to make him *want* to do it. Persuade him that you're working in *his* interests, and the task will get done.

Definite statements, unless you're absolutely sure of them, can get you into trouble, too. Again, an opening like "I believe. . ." or "It's my opinion that. . ." or "Don't you agree that. . ." can save much face later on. Even if you know you're right, soften your statement with one of these statements. I believe it was Samuel Butler who said, "There is no mistake so great as that of being always right."

You'll make people like you as never before if you cultivate the habit of approaching them with the attitude of "Oh, there you are" instead of "Look, here I am!" If you have to ask for information, they'll love you if you ask for some that (you know) they can give. People don't like to say, "I don't know" (as mentioned a few paragraphs ago) and they won't be too happy if you force them into it.

What all this boils down to is attempting to make other peoples' interests your interests. If you realize that other people have the desire to win as strongly as you have, you'll never be a bad loser. I know people who get terribly upset over losing any petty game or competition. Well, bad losers are selfish people, and they show it in this way.

Be happy for the winner. What the heck, you'll have your day soon, and you'll want the loser to be glad for you. Nobody particularly likes a bad loser, or a constant complainer. Try to praise your competitor, and you'll be respected for it. Knock him, and you won't be believed anyway. Mark Twain said, "Good breeding consists in concealing how much we think of ourselves and how little we think of the other person." (Someone said, "Every time a friend succeeds, I die a little." The key is to hide those feelings.)

Being Well Informed Helps

Your overall personality is altered and shaped by your general knowledge, your awareness of the world around you. Are you practical-minded; can you figure things out logically? Do you read at least half as many nonfiction as fiction books? Do you *make* the time to listen to good music occasionally, or to worthwhile lectures? Do you know at least a little about art? The answer to these questions should be "yes" if you want a well-rounded personality.

Of course, we all have our special abilities and particular fields of knowledge. However, you can't talk about these abilities or remain in the company of others who are familiar with the same fields of knowledge all the time. So try to enlarge your scope. There's no reason to be left out of any conversations because you know absolutely nothing about the subject being discussed.

Can you answer most of the following questions? Try.

1. Which baseball team won the World Series in 1989? 1988?
2. Who was the Soviet Premier before Gorbachev?
3. A woman goes into the butcher store. She sees a $.25 piece on the counter, and slips it into her purse. She then buys some meat which costs $.19. She gives the butcher his own quarter. He gives her $.06 change, and her meat. When the woman is outside, she suffers a twinge of conscience and returns to undo her petty thievery. How much money does she return to the butcher?
4. Who starred in both Broadway shows, *Two for the Seesaw* and *The Miracle Worker*?

5. Is *The Memory Book* a work of nonfiction or fiction?
6. Who composed *Rhapsody in Blue*?
7. Can you name at least two states that border Kansas?
8. Is "Scrabble" the name of a food, a game, a car or a movie?
9. Assume that fleas in a jar double themselves every second. Start with 2 and you have 4 in one second, 8 in the next second, and 16 the following second, etc. The jar is exactly half full of fleas in 51 seconds. How many seconds before the jar is full?
10. It's possible to tell if a person is honest by the shape of his ear lobes. True or false?
11. Who ran for the presidency opposite Harry Truman the first time Truman was elected?
12. Once a trade name becomes famous or known, the company need not advertise any longer. True or false?
13. "Oregano" is an opera, a state, or an herb?
14. Which are usually more accurate, slow or fast workers?
15. What is the name given to the man who is seated on a horse and carries a lance at a bull fight? Matador, toreador, banderillo, picador?
16. Does iron have more of a tendencey to crack than steel?
17. Can you think of the names of presidents of the United States beginning with the following letters: A, T, L, C, V, R, E?
18. Who painted *"The Blue Boy?"*
19. Who wrote *Crime and Punishment* and *The Brothers Karamazov*?
20. Which is the better hand, a "straight flush" or a "full house"?
21. Which is the capital city of Maryland? Annapolis, Baltimore, Havre de Grace or Chevvy Chase?

Most of the questions are general knowledge, and a few are on logic, or what you might call practical-mindedness. How do you think you did? If you're not sure, here are the answers:

1. Oakland A's; L.A. Dodgers (in five).
2. Yuri Andropov.
3. Just what she stole — $.25.
4. Ann Bancroft.
5. Nonfiction.
6. George Gershwin.
7. Missouri, Oklahoma, Nebraska, Colorado.
8. A game.
9. One more second; 52 seconds all told.
10. False.
11. Thomas Dewey.

12. False.
13. An herb.
14. Fast workers.
15. Picador.
16. Yes.
17. Adams, Taft, Lincoln, Coolidge, Van Buren, Roosevelt, Eisenhower.
18. Gainsborough.
19. Fyodor Dostoyevsky.
20. A straight flush.
21. Annapolis.

If you have six or more wrong answers, I'd suggest you do a little more reading, or have more discussions on diversified subjects.

All in all, personality consists of getting along with people. I've often read that the majority of people who can't hold on to their jobs very long usually leave or are fired because they couldn't get along with the other personnel, not because they weren't capable of handling the technical part of their work.

I can only leave this subject with the following quote by Daniel Frohman: "Half the secret of getting along with people is consideration of their views; the other half is tolerance in one's own views."

Chapter 18

How To Be an Effective Public Speaker — Without Fear

The nervous speaker was introduced after dinner. He approached the microphone and began haltingly: "My f-f-friends, when I arrived h-here this evening only God and I knew what I was going to say. Now — only God knows!"

It has been suggested that I include a little discussion on public speaking in this book. I suppose you would consider that an aspect of personality. So if you ever have to get up in front of a group to talk, you may find this chapter of some interest.

As far as nervousness is concerned, I can't really help you too much — except perhaps to remind you that you probably wouldn't have been asked to speak unless it was thought that you knew your subject. Just fix it in your mind that if anyone in your audience knew the subject better, he or she would be at the podium, and you'd be listening to him or her.

Of course, if you're ever in the position of having to talk about something you know very little about, I wouldn't blame you for being nervous. Don't allow yourself to be put in that position, and you'll have nothing to be anxious about.

At the risk of sounding repetitious, I must again bring out that if you aren't too interested in yourself—how *you* will sound, whether the audience will like *you*, and so on—you will rarely get nervous. Don't take yourself too seriously, and you'll do fine. In most cases, your talk will be listened to, a few comments like "He's right" or "I disagree with him" will be made, and that will be the end of it. Too many of us insist on inflating the importance to others of things that just aren't that important to them.

How Long Should You Speak?

In my opinion, the most important thing in giving a talk is timing. The thing you *should* be nervous about is boring your audience, and the surest way to do that is to talk *too long*. I've heard many speeches in my time — speeches at company affairs, testimonial dinners, rallies, charity drives and fund raisers — and 70 per cent of them were much too lengthy.

The biggest offenders, I think, are the people who introduce the speakers. Too often, the introduction is longer than the main speaker's talk. If the speaker is an important personality, and well known to everyone present, little introduction is needed. Just his or her name will do.

Perhaps one anecdote pertaining to the speaker may be apropos —*if* you've checked it with him in advance. If the speaker is not well known, state his qualifications quickly and succinctly, and leave the rest to him. Don't become hypnotized by the sound of your own voice!

The most difficult thing to do when giving a talk is to come to a period. You've got to learn to do that or you'll lose the audience. At many functions, speakers are given the amount of time they are not to exceed. They know this beforehand, and yet many of them go blithely over their time limit. They think that what they have to say is so important, and they say it so well, that it's okay for them to break the rule. If they think an audience that's collectively looking at its watches every few minutes is an attentive or happy one, they're mistaken.

Stand up — speak up — shut up! There's the rule to follow. Get up, make your point as emphatically as you want to, then sit down. Perhaps we ought to use the system that an African tribe uses. They make their speakers stand on one leg throughout their talks.

Once the other leg touches the ground, the speaker must stop; in mid-sentence, if necessary (or spears are thrown!).

Will Rogers was once toastmaster at a dinner where each speaker was allotted ten minutes. One man droned on and on for over an hour. At the end of his marathon, he apologized to Will, saying that he'd left his watch at home. Mr. Rogers answered in a loud stage whisper, "There's a *calendar* right behind you."

Preparing and Delivering the Speech

As for the speech itself, I would suggest that you never try to memorize it word for word. If you do, and you forget one word, that's when the hemming and hawing starts. Even if you don't forget part of it, your speech will *sound* memorized, and that tends to alienate your listeners.

Another thing that can make the attention of the audience wander is reading your speech. You might just as well photocopy it and hand it out to them to read at their leisure. That would save a lot of time. Also, if you're reading it, you may lose your place, and then you're really in trouble.

That seems to rule out everything but the completely extemporaneous speech, doesn't it? Well, not quite. Few speeches are ever completely extemporaneous, or "off the cuff." Every speaker has in mind certain points which he wants to get across to his audience. If he makes no preparation at all, many of these points may be forgotten.

I think that the best way to prepare your speech is to lay it out thought for thought. List the thoughts you wish to communicate on a piece of paper in sequence, and let these be your notes for the entire speech. In this way you're not memorizing word for word, yet you're not speaking extemporaneously either.

You know what you want to say about each idea or you wouldn't be introducing it in the first place. As you speak, all you have to do is glance down at your notes each time you've finished speaking on one point. Go to the next point and so on to the conclusion of the talk. One thing you should definitely prepare, or have clearly in mind, is the conclusion. Remember — you must come to a period or you'll go on and on and on.

The ending of your speech is probably the most important part of it, the part most remembered by your audience simply because it's the last thing they will hear you say. If you have a strong anecdote that slams home your final point, fine. If not, keep your strongest point for the end and deliver it with something of a flourish. Let them know you've ended.

It has always been my belief that a speech, whether it be formal or informal, should be entertaining. However, that does not mean that you need become a comedian. If you can't tell jokes or anecdotes well, don't tell them! But if you possibly can, get a little humor into your talk. Make the audience smile or laugh occasionally, and they'll be more interested in the serious parts of the speech.

How to Behave on Any Platform

Aside from the actual content of the talk, the most important consideration is you — the way you speak and the impression you make upon the audience. I can only advise you that the best thing to do is to be as natural as you can. Don't stand at the lectern stiffly. Move and gesture once in a while, so the audience can move their eyes.

Try not to speak in a monotone. Put emphasis on certain words. If you don't give the people in your audience a chance to shift their eyes, or to smile or laugh, or give them a different range of sound, they will make up for this by moving restlessly in their chairs, coughing or talking, and in general losing interest.

Don't be too concerned over the fact that you're nervous *before* your talk. Almost every good and experienced performer or speaker has this problem. There would be something amiss if you *weren't* a bit nervous and tense before facing an audience. Once you're on, that nervousness will disappear.

A trick used by many speakers is to catch the eye of one person at a time and imagine they're speaking to him or her only. That's a good idea, since it keeps you from staring over everybody's head, or gazing continuously at your notes. Incidentally, if you wish to eliminate notes altogether, I've shown you how to do that — how to memorize the thoughts you wish to speak about, in sequence — in the chapter on memory (Chapter 15).

So keep your talk short and to the point; try to get some humor into it; and come to a definite ending. Don't be monotonous. Speak with some authority and look at your audience. If you have to take a breath, take it. There's no need to rush ahead breathlessly. As a matter of fact, a (pregnant) pause at the proper time is quite effective.

There are some more points which may seem obvious, but it's amazing how many speakers overlook them. Don't use long, complicated words when simple, short ones will suffice. Be careful about the use of technical terms or phrases, unless you're speaking to people who are in the same business or profession and can understand the terms. If you must use them to a general audience, define them so that your listeners can follow you.

It's important to realize that the best way to get a point across is to call upon your audience's knowledge and experience rather than your own. To use an analogy pertaining only to your particular field of knowledge will leave the listeners confused. They'll still be thinking about it when they should be listening to your next point. This, incidentally, is also valid when you're having a conversation with only one or two people.

You *can* get up and talk in front of an audience — though you can probably think of many reasons why you can't, including: "I'm too shy," "I've never done it before," "I don't speak well," "I'm afraid I'll look like a fool," and so forth.

Well, remember this — if you wait until all objections are overcome, you'll never attempt anything. Thomas Bailey Aldrich said, "They fail, and they alone, who have not striven." Sure, you may fail as a public speaker, but you'll never know if you don't try it. The reason people don't try new things is the fear of failure, but you can't go through life without facing new things occasionally. Of course, if you never make an effort you'll never fail — but you'll stagnate; that's for sure.

So, if you have to make a speech, don't worry about it too much. Follow the suggestions in this chapter, and do the best you can. Your second speech will be better than your first, and your third will be better than the second. You can only improve as you keep trying.

As a pattern to follow in delivering most speeches, the following lines by the poet Dr. Leifchild, might be appropriate:

> Begin low, speak slow;
> Take fire, rise higher;
> When most impressed,
> Be self-possessed;
> At the end wax warm;
> And sit down in a storm.

Chapter 19

Worry Control — The Secret of Peace of Mind

Build for yourself a strongbox,
Fashion each part with care;
When it's strong as your hand can make it,
Put all your troubles there;
Hide there all thought of your failures,
And each bitter cup that you quaff;
Lock all your heartaches within it,
Then sit on the lid and laugh.

BERTHA ADAMS BACKUS

Wouldn't it be wonderful if we could all build ourselves such a strongbox — a place to pack away our worries, fears, failures, and disappointments? Then again, wouldn't that make all of us completely irresponsible? It may be all right to have a "light head," and not worry about anything, or be afraid of nothing — but that's going to the other extreme, don't you think?

The stress and strain of our current way of life makes it almost inevitable that we harbor some doubts, fears and worries. Dr. Theodore Van Dellen has written that, "The person who fears the modern tempo of living must choose between stress and stagnation."

147

I guess, as with everything else, we just have to learn to attain a happy medium. Worry has been described as the mental capacity for inaction. It is essentially *a fear reaction over a future event which may never materialize.* Of course, if you keep yourself occupied mentally and physically, there isn't much time to worry. However, since most of us do worry, I should devote a little space to the problem.

Paying Interest on Trouble Before It Comes Due

I know that telling you not to worry is about the same as advising you not to breathe. I can, however, try to show you why, in most instances, your worries are wasted effort. They do you absolutely no good, and can harm you.

Worry is a good example of squandered or noncreative imagination. Instead of using your imagination to help you create new ideas, or to improve yourself, you're using it to no apparent purpose. W. R. Inge said that worry is interest paid on trouble before it becomes due.

There is time enough to fret and wring your hands when the expected trouble actually appears — why worry about it now? Don't you realize that most of the things you worry about never happen anyway?

Prove it to yourself! Can you sit down right now and list all the things you were worried about, say, a year ago today? Try it — and I'm sure you won't remember too many, if any at all. While you have the pencil and paper out, list the things you're worried about right now. Put the list in a safe place, and check it a few months or a year from now. Again, you'll find that most of the things you dreaded never happened; or if they did, they weren't so bad as you thought they'd be.

If you make up your mind right now that most of the things you worry about won't occur anyway, and that the worry itself is more painful and agonizing than the event you're worried about, you're on your way to as close to a worry-free existence as is possible nowadays.

It may take a bit of intestinal fortitude to admit to yourself that it is impossible to go through life without some pain, failure, disappointment or frustration. But you might just as well admit it because you know that it's so. Schopenhauer wrote that, "A certain amount of care or pain or trouble is *necessary* for every man at all times. A ship without ballast is unstable and will not go straight."

The thing to do is to learn to accept annoyances of this type. They're inevitable anyway, so what have you got to lose? I know some people who welcome a certain amount of frustration or failure as a challenge — it gives them a "kick" to overcome it and head toward success.

Stop fretting over things that must be. Let's face it — there isn't much you can do about it when it's snowing — except wear boots. And there isn't much you can do about a tooth that must come out — except have it yanked.

I made up my mind years ago that I had no time for worrying. If I get a toothache, I don't worry about it until I can't bear the pain any longer, as I used to do. At the first twinge, I'm on my way to the dentist. No sense putting off the inevitable; you've got to go sooner or later — so I go sooner and avoid a lot of fear and anxiety.

Face the Worst — and You Can Meet Anything

Another trick I use to avoid worry is this: whenever something comes up that may cause trouble, I immediately think of the *worst* that can happen. As soon as I've visualized that, I prepare myself accordingly, then forget about it.

If I've made an investment which looks as if it may turn into a loss, I make up my mind that I'm going to lose the *entire* investment. Of course, I'll try my darnedest to salvage what I can, but if it *is* a total loss — well, I expected it, and that's that. If it turns out well, or if the loss is not too bad (as is usually the case), then it's a pleasant surprise, and I haven't wasted time worrying about it.

So, instead of worrying without rhyme or reason, so to speak — regardless of what's worrying you, *what's the very worst that can happen?* If the worst is not death, or the end of the world, prepare for it in the best way you can — then forget it!

If it *is* death or the end of the world, you've really got nothing to worry about!

I know of one man who used to worry dreadfully about one thing. He traveled on business, and he had heard of several people getting attacks of appendicitis on such trips!

This bothered him terribly. He kept worrying about the business he'd lose if this happened to him. Also, since he wouldn't be near his own doctor, the thought of a strange doctor operating on him worried him something awful.

Well, the worst that could happen, he thought, would be to be away from home at a very busy time and get an appendicitis attack. So during a slow period in his business, he went to his own doctor and had his appendix removed! He doesn't worry about *that* anymore!

This, as I'm sure you realize, is going to somewhat of an extreme. However, I think it brings out my thought about facing the worst, and then preparing for it.

There's got to be some frustration, "lest," as Shakespeare said, "too light winning make the prize light." When the frustration presents itself, realize that it is a necessary part of life, and it won't bother you half so much as it does now. William G. Milnes, Jr. was quoted in the *Saturday Evening Post* as saying, "You're on the road to success when you realize that failure is merely a detour."

I use this quote to stress again, as I have elsewhere in the book, that too many of us too often worry about failure, and in so doing never really try for success. Worrying about failure is the most asinine thing I can think of, *if* it keeps you from trying. If it motivates you to try to avoid the failure, fine. But, again, don't waste too much time worrying about it. Go ahead and start — once you do, you'll handle automatically any little failures that appear.

Sidney Smith said that, "A great deal of talent is lost in the world for want of a little courage. Every day sends to their graves obscure men whom timidity prevented from making a first effort; who, if they could have been induced to begin, would in all probability have gone great lengths."

I think that says it better than I could. "I can't" or "I'm afraid I'll fail" will never get you off the ground. "I'll try" can put you into orbit! Have I made my point? Worrying over possible failure won't avoid the failure. If you must worry about it, let your worry be the starting point for action. Whatever you're afraid *may* happen, prepare or plan for it, and you'll not have to worry about it any more.

I am a great believer in planning for the unexpected. I know that a little extra effort on my part can sometimes avert months of needless worry. No sense being a pessimist; but being a "cockeyed optimist" can be just as bad. The thing to do is to have a realistic attitude, and make up your mind that things do not always go as planned. (Just when you've made your plans, *life* happens!)

Handling Those Everyday Worries

Many of us who haven't any really big problems will spend count-less hours worrying about little things. So plan for those minor dilemmas and stop worrying about them.

If you're leaving for an appointment, start earlier — why worry about being late?

If you're driving into a strange area, get a map or good instructions — why worry about getting lost?

If one of your tires is nearly bald, get a new one now (you'll have to soon anyway) — why worry about getting a flat?

If you're not sure your teeth are in good condition, get them checked — why worry about getting a toothache?

Of course, if these little things don't worry you, that's fine. But according to Dan Bennett, "A man doesn't have any real wisdom until he thinks about indigestion before he eats instead of after-wards."

Preparing for the unexpected (without going to extremes) can be quite useful for eliminating minor (and sometimes major) worries. Many years ago I used two specially built blackboards and two easels for my lectures. They were kept in specially built cases, in the trunk of my car. I used to worry about what would happen if I ever lost them; if the car was stolen or if the blackboards or easels broke. I got rid of this worry very easily. I had another set of boards and easels made, which I kept at home. I haven't had to use them yet — but I don't worry about them any more either! (I haven't car-ried blackboards for over a quarter of a century. My talk — and demonstrations — are in my mind and in my attache case.)

So you see, you may not be able to avert minor worries from time to time, but you can put a stop to their habit of lingering and grow-ing and festering.

When it comes to major worries — family difficulties, financial troubles, things of that nature — many of the rules expressed here still apply. Of course, if the worry is over something that can't *possibly* be eradicated or cured, I can only suggest you stop running full tilt and head on into stone walls. Make up your mind that the situa-tion is inevitable and go on the best way you can. There's an old Chi-nese proberb that goes: "You cannot prevent the birds of sorrow from flying over your head, but you can prevent them from building nests in your hair."

On the other hand, if you're very worried about something that has a possible solution, the best advice I can give you is that given by Dr. George Stevenson in a wonderful little pamphlet called *How to Deal with Your Tensions.* He said, in part: "When something worries you, talk it out. Don't bottle it up. Confide your worry to some levelheaded person you can trust; your husband or wife, father or mother, a good friend, your clergyman, your family doctor, a teacher, school counselor, or dean. Talking things out helps to relieve your strain, helps you to see your worry in a clearer light, and often helps you to see what you can do about it."

But If You Must Worry, Get It Off Your Chest

It's difficult to add much to that; except perhaps to stress the value of talking your worry out, not only to get it off your chest, but to someone who knows more than you, who may be of some help. I'm sure you've heard or read about people who ruined their lives because of things that could easily have been straightened out had they only talked to someone who understood their particular worries or problems.

Don't take advice, of course, from people who know only as much as, or less than, you do about a certain problem. I'm reminded of an acquaintance who was suffering from an annoying and painful skin irritation. A well-meaning friend told him to cover the afflicted area with iodine. This did not improve the condition, and it gave him a third-degree burn to boot. The wiser thing would have been to visit a doctor.

Now — to go from the extreme to the ridiculous — are you the kind of person who drags through life always worrying about things like: Did I set the alarm clock? Did I put out the lights? Did I turn off the oven? Did I unplug the iron? Did I put out the garbage? Did I lock the door?

Of course, the best way to help you to avoid these minor worries is to tell you to learn to remember. Learn to remember to do these things, and you won't have to worry about them. At the risk of sounding commercial, I can only advise you to pick up a copy of one of my books on the subject. Absentmindedness is really a memory problem, and I've gone into detail on this in a few of my books. Or read the chapter in this book on habits. Get into the habit of doing things in their proper order and proper time, and you won't have to worry about them.

To adhere strictly to the subject of worry — just *stop* worrying about these things, will you? If you forget to lock your door, and the house is burgled, I assure you you'll never leave it open again. If you are late to work once because you didn't set your alarm, the odds are you won't make that mistake again.

The point is, the best attitude for you to cultivate if you're really plagued with this type of worry is — "So what!" If you're wrong once or twice, you'll know better or do better next time. Again, what's the worst that could happen? If the worst, in your opinion, is really bad, then take the time to check on the thing you're worried about.

If you've been worrying about whether you put the lights out, in your home or car — well, the worst is that you'll need a battery charge for the car, or your electric bill will be a few cents more. It's up to you to decide whether that's worth worrying about. If a few cents more on your electric bill doesn't matter too much, why worry?

The Last Thing to Worry About

Well, okay — what else do you worry about? Getting old? Oh, yes, that's something many of us worry about. Benjamin Franklin said, "All would live long, but none would be old." How true! Why worry about getting older (older, not old) — think of the alternative!

Anyway, how do you know that old age is not the finest and most rewarding part of life? In this case, it would be wise to look forward to the inevitable. I don't mean to sit and wait for old age, but neither do I mean to worry about it. Prepare for it? Sure. Work out a retirement or pension fund; get interested in hobbies, in which you can participate when you're older, if you like. But, for heaven's sake, don't worry about it! According to Dr. Theodore R. Van Dellen, "Growing old is not so much of a problem as the fear of being old."

And Harry Golden, in his best-seller, *Only In America,* had a good thought on the subject. He suggested that you start each day with the thought in mind that you will live forever. "Start a major alteration on your house at the age of seventy, and at seventy-five enter upon a whole new course of study or learn a new language. Just keep going as though it will never end. And when it does come, you'll hardly notice it."

What else? Are you worried about sickness? Go to your doctor — let *him* worry about it!

Worried about going insane? Good! People who worry about going crazy rarely do!

And don't worry too much about going to hell — you've been there!

Chapter 20

How To Conquer Fear — and Overcome Inevitable Troubles

I have no other foe to fear save Fear.

FREDERICK LAWRENCE KNOWLES

There is not much to differentiate worry and fear. Actually, it's a case of the boil (worry) coming to its painful head (fear). Again, I can't advise you merely to cut out fear completely. Not only is that impossible, but it isn't wise.

Erich Fromm once wrote: "*Rational* anxiety due to the awareness of *realistic* dangers operate in the service of self-preservation; it is an indispensable and healthy part of our psychic organizaton. The absence of fear is a sign of either lack of imagination and intelligence, or a lack in one's will to live." (The italics are mine.)

Rational anxiety or fear of realistic dangers, of course, is an essential part of living. Fear, like pain, can be a warning of, a protection against, imminent danger. If you had no fear of fire, sooner or later you'd probably be badly burned. I could give you a thousand examples, but I'm sure it isn't necessary.

Knowledge brings awareness, and being aware must in some cases incite fear. So, I guess the more you know, the more there is to be afraid of. This is no reason to look askance at knowledge, because no matter how you look at it, ignorance is not bliss.

Many fears, of course, are instilled in us during childhood; and a good thing, too. The burned child fears the fire; although naturally that fear is instilled through the pain of an accident, not by some-one inflicting a burn.

Fear can also be a good creative force. It was the fear of ignorance that created schools; the fear of food poisoning that caused safer and healthier methods of preparing and packaging; the fear of acci-dents that caused safety measures to be applied to buildings, facto-ries and automobiles.

How often have you passed a bad accident on the road, and driven slower and more carefully for at least the next twenty miles? Or heard of someone getting a dread disease, and run to your doctor for the checkup you had put off for such a long time?

In these instances, your fears did you no harm. On the contrary, they may have done some good. It's the abnormal and unreasonable fears that we must get rid of.

The most universal fear of all is the fear of death — fear of the death of oneself or of loved ones. This fear must touch all of us at one time or another. The only way I can think of easing this fear a little is to remind you that it seems silly to fear or anticipate the inevitable. Shakespeare, as usual, said it beautifully, in the tragedy of Julius Caesar:

Cowards die many times before their deaths;
The valiant never taste of death but once.
Of all the wonders that I yet have heard,
It seems to me most strange that men should fear;
Seeing that death, a necessary end,
Will come when it will come.

Know Your Fears — and Make Them Your Tools

Nobody is without fear — no normal person, that is. The greatest and bravest heroes will tell you honestly that when they did their heroic deeds they were as frightened as you or I might have been. The difference is that they were able to overcome that fear — they resisted the urge to give in to it.

You may have to face many things or situations that frighten you. Don't be ashamed of your fear, but practice resisting it, overcoming it. As a matter of fact, one adage for eliminating fear is: "Do the thing you fear."

Many things that you fear now can, believe me, be faced squarely, and even eventually enjoyed. You may be terrified of getting onto a pair of ice skates, but if you face that terror, and learn to skate, you may find you've been missing something pleasurable all these years.

Don't hide your fears from yourself. Harry Emerson Fosdick said, "To get our fear out into the open and frankly face it is of primary importance." You'll never be able to do anything at all about a fear that is not brought out so you can look it squarely in the eye.

Fear of failure? Well, I've discussed that in the preceding chapter. I can only repeat that people who are terrified of failure are the ones who usually are failures, since they're afraid of trying. Make up your mind that the real sign of success is not a straight unmarked line to achievement, but the manner in which you overcome failures!

As far as I'm concerned, if your thoughts lean too heavily to the side of "I might not succeed," you'll never start at all — and that's the worst crime of all. Start — and aim high. As Joel Hawes once said, "Aim at the sun, and you may not reach it, but your arrow will fly far higher that if aimed at an object on a level with yourself."

Make your fears work for you whenever you can. If you fear failure, you should plan ahead so that you can't fail. Prepare an alternative in case you do fail at first. In this way your fear is helping you, not keeping you from beginning.

I was afraid of people when I was very young. I was terribly shy. I decided to face that fear and do something about it. I started to talk to people whenever I could. I had always felt that I had nothing to contribute, so I tried to entertain them. I tried to make them laugh or show them things they had never seen before. I'm certainly not terrified of people any longer; and I put that original fear to work for me.

Sometimes you've got to pretend or act as if many of your fears didn't exist. Theodore Roosevelt once wrote: "There were all kinds of things of which I was afraid at first, but by acting as if I was not afraid I gradually ceased to be afraid. Most men can have the same experience if they choose."

You can have the same experience of overcoming certain fears. Force yourself to act unafraid, and before you know it, it will be true. This has worked for me for years; there's no reason why it shouldn't help you.

I don't believe that most of us are very frightened of the present. It's usually those imaginary future events that fill us with fear. Here, of course, we're getting back into the "worry" problem. It is very often true that if you take care of the present the future will take care of itself. "How much pain have cost us the evils which have never happened" is as valid today as it was when Jefferson said it many years ago.

Don't you realize that the more you dread tomorrow, the less time and inclination you'll have to face and enjoy today? Stop being afraid of life and you'll enjoy life. After all, we pass this way but once!

You just can't avoid some trouble in life. There's a cliché that says, "Into each life some rain must fall" — but why open your umbrella while the sun is shining?

Keep Two Days a Week Free From Fear

To sum up: If you're afraid of something, don't let it eat away at you. Bring it out into the open so that you can do something about it. Face it, and in most cases you'll realize the fear was childish in the first place.

Nowadays, fear of fatal diseases — cancer, heart trouble and so on — causes more anxiety than anything else, I suppose. If that fear makes you get a physical checkup occasionally, that's all to the good. But don't harbor unreasonable dreads.

There's a story about a man who went to see his doctor because he thought he had cancer. The doctor asked him if he had any pain. "No," said the frightened patient. "Well, have you been losing weight consistently?" asked the doctor. The patient replied that he hadn't; as a matter of fact, he'd put on a pound or two. "Then what makes you think you have cancer?"

"I read somewhere that cancer can start with no symptoms at all, and that's exactly what I have!"

I think that more sickness may be caused by the dread of incurable disease than by the disease itself. Sure, it pays to be careful, and to have regular check-ups, but if you are and you do, you're doing all you can, so forget about it. Don't spend so much time avoiding trouble that you have no time for anything else.

Do you suffer from kainophobia — the fear of new things? People do, you know, or it wouldn't have been necessary to coin the word. My wife wouldn't get on an airplane for years. She had never flown and she would just as soon leave it at that. Finally, we were offered a deal which would have been sheer folly to refuse. But to accept it, it was necessary that we fly across the country. Well, my wife clenched her fists and prayed silently throughout the trip. To make a long story short, she now virtually refuses to travel any other way; arguing that it's faster than any other mode of travel, more comfortable, and certainly safer than the tremendous amount of mileage we drove through all kinds of hazardous weather.

Stop denying yourself pleasures by being frightened of new things, or of things you've never done before. Try it once, anyway, to find out whether you *should* be afraid. As I wrote in the chapter on learning, don't be a spectator all the time — participate once in a while, and you'll find out that what you were afraid of can really be enjoyed.

Many books are available on the subject of worry and fear, and I know that a psychiatrist can do wonders, if you'll let him, about unreasonable fears. But perhaps the best way to look at them is the way Robert J. Burdette did. He wrote: "There are two days in the week about which and upon which I never worry. Two carefree days, kept sacredly free from fear and apprehension. One of these days is Yesterday — and the other — is Tomorrow."

Chapter 21

Replace Positive Thinking with Positive Doing

Son: *Mom, I don't think I can pass that test I'm taking in school tomorrow.*
Mom: *Now, now, son! Remember — positive thinking!*
Son: *Okay; I'm sure I can't pass it!*

In doing research for this book, I have of necessity read quite a bit about "positive thinking." It seems that positive thinking is *the* thing nowadays. Many people I've spoken to consider it almost a panacea, a cure-all for just about anything. (Bear in mind that I wrote this almost thirty years ago.)

Well, don't misunderstand me: positive thinking is all right — except that in all the books I went through on the subject I didn't read too much about positive *doing*. It is hard to believe that sitting in your room all day and thinking positively is going to do you much good. As a matter of fact, I'm sure that you'll agree that spending all your time considering isn't going to leave much time for accomplishing.

As mentioned earlier, thinking in the present tense is problem-solving. If you're thinking in the past tense, you're remembering — and that's awfully close to reminiscing. Thinking of the future is anticipating — and while anticipating problems can be useful at times, why not concentrate on the ones that need solving now?

So you've got a few problems that are bothering you right now. Then go ahead and do something about them. Sitting around thinking about what you *will* do may put you in the position of never finding out what you can do about them. Certainly I'm not advocating that we should do things without giving them some advance thought, but it seems plausible that if we got rid of some of our *negative* thinking, the positive thinking would take care of itself.

Thoughts Must Become Actions to Work

It's not so easy as it sounds, I know. Many people, I suppose, do need psychiatric help to rid themselves of their negative thoughts. In many cases, however, I can't help feeling that common sense plus a little will power would do it. According to Dr. Karen Horney, "Fortunately analysis is not the only way to resolve inner conflicts. Life itself still remains a very effective therapist." I am, of course, not referring to the severe neurotic, for whom competent help is the best, and perhaps the only, solution.

To the normal person with normal anxieties and tensions, the "normal neurotics" (Dr. George Stevenson maintains that anxiety and tension are essental functions of living, just as hunger and thirst are), I say get off that negative kick. Voltaire would have told you that, "The longer you dwell on your misfortunes, the greater is their power to hurt you."

If you have something to do, don't let indecision plague you. Do it the best way you know how at that moment. Why worry about whether you'll make a mistake or not? Sure, you may make a mistake — then again you may not. And can you think of a better way to learn than from your own mistakes? In most cases, you'll feel better after the thing is done, whether you goofed or not. And keep in mind Dr. William J. Reilly's thought: "The only person who makes no mistakes is the person who does nothing — and that's the greatest mistake of all!"

A happy medium between negative and positive thinking is most desirable. Each can be overdone. For example: don't cultivate the completely pessimistic and self-centered attitude of the person who gets caught in a downpour and thinks, "Why do these things happen *only* to me?"

At the other extreme is the fellow who falls from the twentieth story of a skyscraper, and as he falls past the ninth story, thinks "So far, so good!" How optimistic can you get?

Don't waste time completely in negative thinking, and don't waste *too* much time in positive thinking. A study at Michigan State University proved that you use more brain power and energy in preparing to solve a problem than in the actual solving.

Please don't just agree with me, shaking your head affirmatively, then go right back to doing as you usually do. Make the effort necessary to *try out* these ideas.

If I hadn't believed in them, this book might never have been written. Sure, all the ideas and thoughts were already in my mind, but so were thoughts like: "I don't think I could put them into words! I don't think I could write well enough; I don't know whether people will be interested; I don't know where to start." (Again, I wrote this thirty years ago!)

Well, I solved the last problem very easily. I just *started!* How true that all progress comes from daring to begin. I would still be fighting those negative thoughts if I hadn't simply begun. "He has half the deed done who has made a beginning."

I am a great believer in "learning by doing." Picturing or seeing my ideas as successful books, is always a pleasant thought, but without the *doing* there just wouldn't be any books. I guess the thing to do is to make the thinking and doing work hand in hand. You've got much more going for you that way.

Those Obstacles Are There for a Purpose

To get back to positive doing: Are there many things you would like to do, but are afraid to try for fear of failure? You're afraid that there are too many difficulties involved? Well, here's a place where positive thinking can be of help. Just remember and believe that the surmounting or equalizing of difficulties is *part* of learning something new or different.

If you can make yourself believe this truth emphatically, you'll not worry about difficulties for the rest of your life. And a little analyzing on your part will show you that it's so. Just try to think of anything you have ever accomplished — anything, no matter how trivial or how important. Now try to recall the annoyances or difficulties that you had to overcome in doing it. Honestly now, didn't you learn something from nearly every one of them? Just think about it for a while and you'll surely agree.

W. M. Punshon put it this way: "There are difficulties in your path. Be thankful for them. They will test your capabilities or resistance; you will be impelled to persevere from the very energy of the opposition. But what of him that fails? What does he gain? Strength for life. The real merit is not in the success but in the endeavor; and win or lose, he will be honored and crowned."

But suppose you feel that it's senseless to try a thing because you know it's beyond you — you could never learn to do it well.

Why worry about doing it well? The first thing to *do* is to learn it, even if not well. Learning to do something at all is the springboard to learning it well. Secondly, how do you *know* you can't do it? "I can't" is not a fact, but an idea. A good illustration of this is the old chestnut about the young man who was asked if he could play the piano. His answer was, "I don't know if I can play or not, I've never *tried.*" Now *there* was a well-adjusted young man.

One entire book I read on how to be happy and/or successful could have been trimmed down to a single concise paragraph. It told me to simply see in my mind's eye whatever I desired to happen. If you desire to be a millionaire, see yourself doing the things a millionaire would do. See yourself living, working, acting like a millionaire. In other words, see yourself *as* a millionaire.

Of course, that's just another way of saying, "Think positively." I'm sure what the author meant was that this seeing would lead to doing. However, you can "think thin" with all your might, but if you keep overeating, you're bound to stay fat, or grow fatter.

On this particular subject Shakespeare wrote: "Our doubts are traitors and make us lose the good we often might win by fearing to attempt."

You see what I mean, don't you? Why think that you can't do something before you've tried it? In most cases, you'll surprise yourself once you try. And certainly there is no shame involved in doing something the best you know how, even if you fail. At least you'll know you've tried; then you can turn your thoughts and energies to other things. Your victories will outweigh your failures, I assure you.

But don't think of failure. If you feel you can't, or that you haven't the talent, or if you feel incompetent, perhaps it will help to remember what U.S. Senator George F. Hoar said: "Much of the good work of the world has been that of dull people who have done their best."

Nothing personal intended, of course. The point is, too many good things have been lost to the world because of people fearing to put their ideas into practical action. It shouldn't be necessary for me to remind you of all the great thinkers and inventors who were ridiculed at first, but who persevered over fantastic odds to achieve success. It's a human failing to deride new ideas or efforts. The thing you must do is laugh at the scoffers and go right ahead and do what you feel is right.

Don't get me wrong, I'm not urging you to turn into a nonconformist; that's up to you. I'm just advising you that it might be better to stop worrying about what others think and find out, and concentrate on, what *you* think.

Turning Duties into Exciting Challenges

Some seemingly unpleasant duties that you must perform can be made easier to accomplish if you look at them as challenges. This idea has been, and is, a great help to me. I've used it since childhood, and it certainly works for me. There's no reason why it shouldn't work for you as well.

Try making a mental wager with yourself that you can do this thing, or that you can handle a particular situation with good sense. In my own work, lecturing and entertaining for audiences with my memory demonstration, anything can happen. Through experience, of course, I have learned to handle most eventualities. Occasionally, however, I will find myself performing for a completely unfriendly audience.

Years ago, when I saw an audience that was, let us say, a bit under the weather, my first impulse was to leave. My stomach would start churning; I'd break out into a cold sweat; in other words, I was scared. My thinking ran something like this: "Why should I have to put up with this? After all, I'm a well-paid performer, I don't need this. Why put up with their rudeness for the hour I'm on stage? If they don't want to listen to me, it's their loss, not mine. Why do they bother hiring entertainment if they don't intend to pay attention to it?" (This, of course, is no longer ever a problem for me. I'm a keynote or after-dinner speaker at high-level corporate gatherings.)

I finally realized that this was not only egotistical thinking, but completely useless. It did nobody — mainly me — any good whatsoever. The fact remained that I had to go on. There was more involved than the audience — there were agents, managers, committee chairmen, and so on. I had no choice but to go through with my performance.

The trouble was that I had worked myself up to such a point that I went on stage mad, hating the audience, and of course I lost them completely.

Fortunately, these audiences were, and are, few and far between. But those were the ones I remembered. They stuck in my mind and made me feel awful.

Well, I finally got smart. My present thinking prior to a show for people I think comprise a bad audience is: "Well, most of the audiences I appear for consist of friendly people. It's a pleasure to work for them. This audience will make me appreciate them all the more. But I can handle them! After all, I'm a seasoned performer; this is a test of my mettle; it's a challenge. I won't shirk the challenge I know I can quiet them down. They're all decent, friendly people basically and I know I can sober them up."

What a world of difference! What I realized was that it never had been the audience that beat me; I had defeated myself! I was doing a bad show *before* I stepped in front of the microphone. (I also realize as I read this that *I paid my dues!*)

Looking at the whole thing as a challenge not only made the job easier, but gave me a greater feeling of accomplishment when I came through with a good performance.

I've taken quite a bit of space to tell you some very simple and basic ideas — namely, that positive thinking is fine when it goes hand in hand with positive doing; and that when you have something that must be done, but you think it's an unpleasant duty, make a challenge out of it. In that way, some unpleasant duties can actually give you a finer sense of accomplishment than pleasant or ordinary chores.

Why not make things easier for yourself if you can? Don't let things bother you too much; just do the best you can under the circumstances. One thing though — don't use "the best I can" as an excuse for bad work or poor showings. Too many of us brush things off with "It's the best I can do" and leave things practically undone. So when I say, do the best you can under the circumstances, I mean the *best* you can, not second best. Then you'll never have to look back at it and feel sorry about it. And remember what Oliver Wendell Holmes said: "The great purpose of life is to *live* it."

Chapter 22

What Kind of Success Do You Want?

Success is a prize to be won. Action is the road to it. Chance is what may lurk in the shadows at the roadside.

O. HENRY

There is one sure way for a person to become a millionaire almost overnight and that is to come up with a guaranteed formula for success. How I wish I could come up with a set of instructions that could assure success to its reader or user.

Unfortunately, there is not, and never could be, any such thing. One reason is that there are many schools of thought as to what constitutes success. Does the word "success" mean to be rich, to be famous, to be happy? I don't know myself. I do know that it is quite possible to be rich and/or famous, yet not happy. Then again, there are many fortunate people who are neither rich nor famous, but are happy.

Success is strictly a personal concept. There are those who feel they could not be happy unless they became famous or wealthy, or both. Those who can attain happiness without fame or wealth are indeed fortunate and are to be envied. It's all in the mind. It is possible to be happy under almost any circumstances, if your mind allows it. And who's to say that being happy is not being successful?

Don't Measure Success Backward

I've always been a little concerned (and amused) over the fact that we too often measure success backward. We set up examples of what we consider successful people, and then try to imitate them. It's mass syllogistic thinking again. Let me give you an example:

Mr. Z was a full-time chicken plucker at the age of eight. Mr. Z is now a very wealthy and/or famous man. Therefore, if you want to become wealthy and famous, it is a good idea to be a full-time chicken plucker at the age of eight.

This sounds pretty funny; but sometimes the laugh's on us. I know many people who think like that, knowingly, and still others who do so subconsciously. We do it with regard to almost any kind of achievement. Not long ago I read a newspaper story about a man who was 105 years old. When asked to what he attributed his longevity, he answered that he never drank or smoked. Being a somewhat heavy smoker, I started to cut down immediately!

I even stopped smoking altogether for a while, until I read about another man who was 110 years old! In his interview, he bragged about the fact that he'd been smoking since he was fifteen years of age. Well, I've been smoking again since then. (Not for the past six years.)

I'm not trying to advise anyone as to whether to smoke or not, you understand — I'm just trying to demonstrate how success of any kind is usually measured backward.

Professor Einstein failed a mathematics entrance exam when he was sixteen; Abe Lincoln split logs when he was a young man; Glenn Cunningham, the great runner, was burned so badly when he was a child he was told he'd never walk again.

These people are all to be admired, but I don't think we can use their lives as examples. There must be thousands of scientists or mathematicians who did not fail entrance exams; not every man who became president had to live in a log cabin when he was a boy; and I'm sure that there are many female movie stars who did not have to be "nice" to producers to get where they are! That a man has never smoked is not necessarily the reason he's lived to be 105. What about all the people who never smoked and who died young?

Please don't think that at any age you can purchase paints, brushes and canvas and, because Grandma Moses never took an art lesson and became a famous painter late in life, you can too! There may indeed be another Grandma Moses out there, but for most of us lessons and long study are necessary before we can paint anything worthwhile.

Some people seem to think that the one way to be successful is to imitate another successful person at his present state of success. That may work occasionally, but usually it won't, and what's more, the imitators are usually considered just that — imitators.

Yes, you should learn from others, but imitating them seldom leads to success. Too often, nowadays, success is measured not by what we give to society, but rather by what we can take from it. It's the same story — keep others in mind, think of what you can contribute to society, and your chances of being successful will be greatly increased.

You Are More Successful Than You Realize

If you feel you're not getting anywhere in life, stop complaining about your bad luck. It has always been my strong belief that *ability* (or talent) *seeks its own level.*

If you have the ability you must, eventually, rise to the level of society where that ability belongs. If you don't have it, you'll never reach that level until you've acquired the necessary ability. I, personally, have always agreed with James M. Barrie's philosophy that, "Not in doing what you like, but in liking what you do is the secret of happiness."

This can be paraphrased to show one difference between success and happiness: "Success is getting what you want. Happiness is wanting what you get." However, it would seem to me that there is no reason not to mix a bit of each. If you can attain some measure of what you want, *and* be happy with it after you've attained it — well, friend, you've got it made!

So now your complaint is that if you could just attain a little success, you'd be happy with it — isn't it? Well, I don't believe you! I don't think you are being truthful with yourself. I'm willing to bet that you have already attained some measure of success. Stop to think about it for a moment. I'm right, am I not? In some way or other, you have attained some sort of success!

Being alive and thinking is success! I once heard a lecture on metaphysics in which the lecturer said, "The age of miracles is certainly not gone — *you* are a miracle!" Now then, if you agree that you have attained some measure of success, are you happy with what you've already accomplished?

If you aren't, don't fret! It's quite normal. To be completely and wholly satisfied is to start dying. There just wouldn't be anything else to look forward to. Everybody has some feelings of insecurity. That, too, is normal. It was Dwight D. Eisenhower who said that, "The best example of perfect security is a man who is serving a life sentence in prison." If a man is serving a life sentence, and knows definitely that there is no hope for parole, and if he has no family outside to think and worry about, he's got complete security — and is also a good example of living death.

So stop worrying about reaching complete security, or complete success — there is no such thing. Even if there were, we wouldn't really want to attain it. Why should we, when the real enjoyment and thrill of living comes from working toward some goal? Spanish writer Cervantes said it very simply many years ago: "The road is always better than the inn."

I'm sure that many times you've striven for some particular goal, finally attained it, and then lost interest — immediately substituting another goal.

If you always seem to be harboring a slight feeling of insecurity, that's nothing serious. As a matter of fact, you're better off than if you did not have any feeling of insecurity. It's that very feeling that forces you to seek out success, to set your goals higher each time, and that gives you the incentive. William Feather said that, "Insecurity is the chief propulsive power in the world."

You understand, of course, that when I write of success, I'm referring to individual success in your own chosen field.

Having Trouble Meeting the "Right" People?

Too often, I hear people complain that they have no particular or outstanding ability; or that they don't know the right people; or that they've tried and tried and keep failing; or that they have no luck — so they might as well give up. In answer to the first instance, I can only repeat what H. J. Heinz replied when asked the secret of his success: "To do a common thing uncommonly well brings success." So you see, no matter what you do, if you learn to do it uncommonly well, you'll have an oustanding ability.

If you feel that you are being held back because you don't know the right people, you're merely setting up a good excuse for yourself. Remember: "Ability seeks its own level." If you have the ability, the "right" people will seek you out. You may have to make it your business to be in the right place at the right time to help them find you — but they'll find you sooner or later.

But be prepared for a possible disappointment when you do meet the "right" people. They may be searching for someone to help them! In most cases, you're better off if you help yourself than if you wait for others to give you a push. Justice Brandeis was so right when he wrote, "No one can really pull you up very high — you lose your grip on the rope. But on your own two feet you can climb mountains."

Yes! You can climb mountains! If you've tried and failed repeatedly, either try something else or try to find out what you're doing wrong. In any case, try again. I think you'll find it's true that most successes are achieved by 99 percent perspiration and 1 percent inspiration.

Here, positive thinking comes in handy. Try to see your goal, whatever it may be. Picture that little success you're aiming toward, and you'll find it easier to overcome each obstacle that gets in your way. Get a definite picture in your mind of what you're trying to achieve, and you'll have something to work toward.

Instead of grumbling over difficulties and obstacles, make each task or duty an adventure, a challenge. When you finally reach your goal, those obstacles will seem quite trivial to you. Harold Helfer put it this way: "Success is a bright sun that obscures and makes ridiculously unimportant all the little shadowy flecks of failure."

Too many of us are ready to quit too soon and too easily. Nothing worthwhile is ever achieved without a bit of hard work and a few failures. There are many things that cannot possibly be accomplished *without* failures. Keep in mind that little failures multiplied bring success, and you'll feel better about them. Think of trying to open a jar whose cap is stuck. You can force and pry ten times without results; the eleventh try may get that cap off easily. But without those first ten failures, you'd never make it.

If you drive a car, or type, or speak a foreign language — if you are the master of any ability that took time and effort and practice to develop — you've probably forgotten the mistakes and discouragements that were part of the learning process. It is difficult perhaps for you to picture the time when you couldn't drive, type or speak that foreign language. And yet, if you think back, you'll realize that it was a series of mistakes, and minor failures that led to the final accomplishment.

So don't waste time looking for people to help you. I think you'll agree, sooner or later, that the best place to look for a helping hand is usually at the end of your arm. Don't waste more time by continually worrying about whether you're doing the right thing, or whether you ought to do it at all. According to Emerson: "Don't waste life in doubts and fears; spend yourself on the work before you, well assured that the right performance of this hour's duties will be the best preparation for the hours or ages that follow it."

Don't Depend on the Predictions of Others — Make Your Own

What else can I tell you about achieving success? Well, let's see. Although someone once said that "Striving for perfection in all things is an open invitation to failure" — and I agree with him — I also think that you must know your business. Work at it! Many of us think we know something well when we hardly know it at all. Sophocles said that, "One must learn by doing the thing; for though you think you know it, you have no certainty until you try."

Without work there can never be success. Unfortunately, the very thing that can help people who are failures, or who suffer from boredom, laziness, loneliness and what have you, is often the only thing they won't try — *work!*

Charles Kingsley wrote in a letter: "Thank God every morning when you get up that you have something to do that day which must be done, whether you like it or not. Being forced to work and forced to do your best, will breed in you temperance and self control, diligence and strength of will, cheerfulness and content, and a hundred virtues which the idle never know."

So pick a starting point, if you haven't already done so, and work from there. You've got to start someplace. James Watt watched a kettle boiling — that was his starting point. The end result was the steam engine! Isaac Newton saw an apple fall. . .

Starting is not always easy, I know. As a matter of fact, it's the hardest part of achieving success. You'll need all your energy just for the starting; after that you may be able to coast for a while. Only a small percentage of a motor's power is necessary to run your car, but *all* its power may be necessary to start it!

I believe that this is so with *any* task. Did you ever have to clean out a drawer or closet that was full of many years' accumulation of junk? Usually you keep putting the job off time and time again, as the drawer or closet gets worse and worse. You know from your own experience that once you actually get started the job isn't anywhere so bad as you thought it would be. It's the getting started on any project that's the most difficult part of the project.

Glenn Cunningham was once told that he could never walk again, and he became a famous and successful runner. Similarly, many people have been discouraged because of the results of intelligence and capability tests, and still attained success. The results of these tests are not always correct. And even if you don't think you've got the ability, you may have it anyway.

It's like the perfomer who was telling his psychiatrist, "Doc, I can't sing or dance or tell jokes — what should I do?"

Doctor: "Quit show business."

Patient: "But I can't — I'm a star!"

People can take an exam under bad conditions — perhaps they're ill or have something on their minds — and spend the rest of their lives living according to the findings of the unrealistic results. I don't intend to knock I.Q. or aptitude tests, but — let's face it — they aren't always 100 percent reliable. Just recently I read that a group of Eskimoes had been tested, and the results showed definitely that they would not be able to adapt themselves to arctic climates!

The Eskimoes don't know this, and go on living quite happily, and well adjusted to the Arctic. This reminds me of a sign hanging on the wall of a General Motors plant: According to the theory of aerodynamics and as may be readily demonstrated through wind tunnel experiments, the bumblebee is unable to fly. This is because the size, weight and shape of his body in relation to the total wingspread make flying impossible. But the bumblebee, being ignorant of these scientific truths, goes ahead and flies anyway — and makes a little honey every day."

I mention all this for the benefit of those whose confidence may have been shattered because of the negative results of a test at one time or another. Take the test again — you may be surprised. I've met people who for years have exclaimed that they couldn't tolerate, say, roast beef. I then found out that when they had originally tried it years before, the beef had been either bad or improperly prepared. If they had tried it again, under favorable conditions, they might have loved the stuff. Don't let the results of one instance change your life. You may miss out on something good.

If you do have skill, and your confidence in it has been shattered, that skill is wasted. There's a saying that goes "Skill *and* confidence are two soldiers who can conquer armies."

There are a few more thoughts on the subject of success in the next chapter. Right now, let me leave you with this notion over which to ponder: "A poor man can be happy, but no happy man is poor!"

Chapter 23

How to Make Your Own Good Luck

*People of mediocre ability often achieve suc-
cess because they don't know enough to quit.*

BERNARD BARUCH

I've tried to tell you a little bit about how I feel about the subject of
success. I hope my thoughts will help you, at least by giving you
something to think about. I realize that the most difficult thing in
the world is to change someone's outlook, one's way of life, one's
ideas.

Let's face it — most will read this book and go on doing and thinking just as they always have. Well, that's as it should be, perhaps.
Who am I to say you'd be better off if you changed? However,
if you've been discontented — if you've been, or are, unhappy
with your lot — some of the ideas in this book may be of some
assistance.

Of course, the only way in which they can be of any help is if
they're *used*. Even if they're exactly opposite to what you've usually
done or thought, try them! If they don't help, forget them — but give
them a chance first. If you find they do help, they will become habit
in no time at all.

175

The way you think is the way you live. Your mind is the ruler of your life — so why not train it to the best of your ability? Your way of thinking, your outlook on life, can overcome any obstacle that possibly presents itself. And never mind telling me that ignorance is bliss — if it was, there would be more ecstatic people in this world!

Are Other People Holding You Back?

Do you feel that people are holding you back, that you have enemies who are keeping you from success? Well, perhaps that's so — although this kind of thinking is usually just an excuse for failure. But, assuming you really do, why not accept the fact that just about everyone has some enemies.

It's unfortunate, certainly, but it's unlikely that anyone could go through life without making at least one foe. If you're in business, or just starting a business, you might as well be prepared for, not necessarily enemies, but certainly competition. Be happy for it! Without competition it wouldn't be much fun trying to reach success.

It's difficult to start at the top in any job or business — unless that job is digging a hole(!), or unless you're fortunate enough to marry the boss's daughter after a really short engagement. So stop blaming your enemies. As a matter of fact, they usually help you! Edmund Burke wrote that, "He that wrestles with us strengthens our nerves and sharpens our skill. Our antagonist is our helper." It's true, you know. Healthy competition and even out-and-out enemies should only make you work better and harder.

Success, it seems, is nothing more than a state of mind. It's all in the way you look at it. Avoid measuring success backward, or measuring it with a warped ruler. It's like the publicity given each year to the "ten best-dressed women" in the world. It has always bothered me a bit because the women chosen are always wealthy ones. I can't see why they should receive any special acclaim since it's certainly no hardship for them to be well dressed. If the ten women chosen as "best dressed" were all of moderate means, that would make more sense. Not having the wealth with which to purchase any clothes they desire; making do with what they have; not being able to afford the advice of top designers and still being well dressed — that's more impressive; that's more like achievement and success.

To get back to basics — back to *you* — has it ever occurred to you that many people have become successful simply by making themselves available? What I mean is, if you think the "big break" is going to seek you out, forget it! You've got to be there when it arrives. Of course, this holds true for any kind of break or opportunity, not only *the* big break.

If you're selling a product, you must see your clients over and over again. Remember that the little failures build up to success. You can see a client perhaps twenty times and not sell him a thing — the twenty-first time you see him may be the time you get the big order that makes all the other visits worthwhile and it probably was the twenty "unsuccessful" visits that eventually caused the breakthrough.

How to Contact People on a Higher Level

Of course, learning to deal with people is an important factor toward making the road to success easier to travel. There've been many hints and suggestions on this subject scattered throughout this book. There is one other little idea or trick that has helped me tremendously through the years. This is for you if you find it difficult to speak to those you think are on a higher social or economic level than you are.

If you find yourself staring in awe and unable to speak intelligently, or perhaps stammering and stuttering, when you are confronted by the big man who may perhaps open some doors for you — if you are the type who always berates himself afterward for acting the fool in front of important people — this idea should be of more than a little help.

Usually, the more important the person is, the easier it is to speak to him or her. But if knowing or believing this doesn't help, here's the little trick. The problem is to manage to get such a person down to what you believe is your level. Once this is done, you can speak to him as you would to a friend. Well, when you walk into a large office and are confronted by an awe-inspiring executive, the first thing to do even as you say "hello," is to picture that person in some *basic human position!*

That's all there is to it. You might picture the person in his or her underwear, for example. I won't go into intimate detail, for obvious reasons! However, I'm sure you have the idea. If you can really picture or visualize the person in this basic human position, you'll have no trouble being yourself, and speaking to that person as you'd like. It's awfully difficult to be awe-inspiring in your underwear!

It took only one paragraph to explain this to you, but don't sell the idea short. It was a great help to me years ago, and there's no reason why it shouldn't help you, too. It puts you on an equal level with anyone. It's like being in a nudist colony. There is no way to tell the executive from the laborer when all outer garments and embellishments are removed.

Just try it; see for yourself. The only problem for me, now, is that when I meet people who've read this and find them staring at me, I'll wonder how the devil they're picturing me!

If you want others to have confidence in you, you must earn that confidence. The little things that are overlooked can be most important when it comes to earning this confidence and trust.

If you've told someone that you'll call at a certain time or on a specific day, do so. If you've told him that you'll mail something that day or be somewhere at a definite time, mail it or be there. Of course, there are always extenuating circumstances, but you can't use them as excuses too often and expect people to have confidence in you, depend on you, or want to do business with you.

Sure there may be (and are) some famous and successful people who can *not* be depended upon. You may know of them *because* they can't be depended on. Don't measure success backward! Those are the exceptions. They didn't become popular because they weren't dependable, they became popular in spite of it. That's the hard way.

Making Your Own Luck

Acquire a reputation for being dependable, and opportunity will keep knocking. Be there to open the door, and you're in! If your argument is that you have no luck, opportunity never knocks for you — cut it out! You're making excuses again. Most successful people will tell you that you must make your own luck. When asked if he believed in luck, Jean Cocteau replied, "Certainly. How else do you explain the success of those you don't like?"

The trouble is that, too often, we apply this excuse even to people we do like. Everyone else's success is due to luck — our failures are all due to bad luck. Well, I doubt it. If you were to find it possible to spend every minute of a few days with someone whose success you ascribe to luck, you would realize that he or she works much harder than you do. If you insist on envying these people, at least envy them for their ability to look opportunities squarely in the face without mistaking them for obstacles or difficulties!

Luck is being ready. Or, according to an old Chinese proverb: "The more you know, the more luck you will have." So, instead of wasting precious time bemoaning your unlucky fate, prepare yourself for luck! That's right — prepare yourself so that when an opportunity does come along, it won't be dissipated because you aren't ready, or don't know enough to take advantage of it.

If you feel you *are* ready and do know enough, then go out and *look* for opportunity — and be sure you can recognize it when you see it. H.L. Mencken said that "People seldom recognize opportunity because it comes disguised as hard work." There is really no substitute for work, you know, so accept the inevitable! Think of how you'll feel after you've worked hard for years, achieved some measure of success, and hear people say, "Aw, he's lucky, that s all!"

I've already talked about how being backed into a corner can sometimes be the best thing that can happen to you. Henry J. Kaiser said almost the same thing: "Trouble is nothing more than opportunity in work clothes."

Nat Cole was a piano player, working in small clubs whenever he could get the bookings. One of the occupational hazards in this type of work is drunks! One evening an occupational hazard kept insisting that Cole sing a song. Nat had never sung in public before, but he was in a spot. The drunk kept insisting noisily; Cole thought he'd better humor him or else cause a free-for-all which could cost him his job. So he sang! This bit of trouble started Nat "King" Cole along the road to one of the most successful singing careers in modern show business!

Years ago, Mary Martin had a nickname on Broadway. She was known as "Audition Mary." Perhaps she had read that Disreali said, "The secret of success is constancy to purpose," and believed it! She sure kept on trying, and learning, even in the face of rebuffs and failures. She could have called it bad luck and given up, and never been heard from again. It took work, time and plenty of intestinal fortitude — tenacity — but she finally got "lucky"! If you still think she was lucky, well you may be able to get lucky too — and probably will — if you work as hard as Mary Martin did, and have the talent, to boot.

Opportunity Never Stops Knocking

Some are of the opinion that they had their chance, perhaps years ago, to become successful. They feel that once an opportunity has been overlooked or wasted, there is no second chance. Nonsense!

There is no allotted number of chances being sparsely handed out, one to a customer. It's only the hordes of failures, who have stopped seeking opportunity after their first chance at it, who have promoted the idea that it knocks only once!

Walter Malone wrote a little poem called *Opportunity* which it might not hurt you to memorize, or at least read, concentrate on and believe.

They do me wrong who say I come no more
When once I knock and fail to find you in;
For every day I stand outside your door
And bid you wake and rise to fight and win.

Wail not for precious chances passed away!
Weep not for golden ages on the wane!
Each night I burn the records of the day —
At sunrise every soul is born again.

Are you a martyr type? Are you really happy when you're in trouble because you like the idea of having people feel sorry for you? Doug Jerrold said, "Some people are so fond of ill luck that they run halfway to meet it." I know people like that who don't realize it themselves. Look into it. I know that this seems silly on first reading — the thought of people actually looking for bad luck — but there are people like that. Make sure you're not one of them!

Instead of complaining about your bad luck, go out and look for good luck by doing something about it. You'll be surprised at how lucky you may get after working hard toward what you wish to attain or accomplish. All the talent, knowledge or skill in the world won't help you any if you don't *use* them. Go out and *act* — do something — don't just sit there!

There are chapters throughout this book that I hope will help you to observe better, understand more, think more clearly, use your imagination and learn from facts — but none of these things can, or will, do you much good if you don't go out and *do* something with them.

You can improve yourself if you really want to, if you're not afraid of a little work. At the beginning of this chapter I said that the most difficult thing for one person to do is to change another person's way of thinking and living. It's true, unfortunately. "Unfortunately" because I know so many people who need not be failures, or at least could be more successful than they are, if they would allow their thinking and living patterns to be altered.

The *Harvard Business Review* once reprinted the letterhead used by a large corporation. It read as follows:

To look is one thing.
To see what you look at is another.
To understand what you see is a third.
To learn from what you understand is still something else.
But to *act* on what you learn is all that really matters.

Well, I've touched on some ideas in this book that I sincerely hope will be acted upon by some, that I sincerely hope will be beneficial to those who do try them and apply them.

Remember that just agreeing with me doesn't help you any. At the risk of seeming repetitious, I must warn you that nodding agreement and doing nothing about it is just as bad as, or worse than, actively disagreeing. And if you're thinking that you will try some of these ideas "someday" — forget it! You'll never get around to it if you don't do it now.

I leave you with this thought of William James: "No matter how full a reservoir of maxims one may possess and no matter how good one's sentiments may be, if one has not taken advantage of every concrete opportunity to *act*, one's character may remain unaffected for the better. With mere good intentions, hell is proverbially paved."

Chapter 24

When to Begin

A violin virtuoso living in America truly believed that he could play so well that he could actually charm a savage beast. Despite the warnings and pleas of his friends, he decided he would go to the jungles of Africa, unarmed, with only his violin to protect him. He stood in a clearing in the dense jungle and began to play. An elephant picked up his scent, and came charging toward him; but when he came within hearing distance, he sat down to listen to the beautiful music.

A hungry cat sprang from a tree with fangs bared but it, too, succumbed to the music. Soon a lion appeared to join the others. Before long, many wild beasts were seated near the virtuoso. He played on, unharmed.

Just then a leopard leaped from a nearby tree onto the violinist, and devoured him! As he stood licking his chops, the other animals approached, and asked, "Why did you do that? The man was playing such lovely music!"

The leopard, cupping his ear, said, "Eh, what'd you say?"

One of the things that I've often repeated throughout this book is the fact that if you don't use, or at least try, the ideas and suggestions, they can't possible do you any good.

The anecdote at the head of this chapter points it out beautifully. Unfortunately, good music means absolutely nothing if it can't be heard. Similarly, the greatest aids and ideas are wasted if they are not used.

As I emphasized in the section on learning, having the wish to do, try or learn anything is not enough. You've got to really *want* to utilize these ideas and suggestions.

Abraham Lincoln said that, "Your own resolution to succeed is more important than any other one thing." If you resolve to *use* the ideas contained herein, they cannot help but aid you in your business, social life and everyday living.

Of course, it's much simpler to fall back into old comfortable habits whenever some sort of obstacle appears. But remember that there wouldn't be much gratification if there were never any obstacles in your path. According to John Neal, "Kites rise against, not with the wind. No man ever worked his passage anywhere in a dead calm."

If you keep in mind that the obstacles more often than not become stepping stones to success, they won't deter you any longer. On the other hand, you must learn to distinguish between insurmountable obstacles and the "stepping stone" variety.

Don't waste time with the insurmountable ones. Try various ways to avoid them. Dr. Theodore R. Van Dellen wrote, "When a situation cannot be altered, don't waste energy being dissatisfied."

Learn to accept the inevitable and you'll save yourself many frustrations and heartaches. You can't have everything, and philosopher Bertrand Russell was so right when he said, "To be without some of the things you want is an indispensable part of happiness."

Let me stress again that most problems *can* be satisfactorily solved, and most goals reached, if you will simply *do* something about them. Don't always wait until you can "see your way clear" — a little action can do wonders for the eyesight. Your activity will create activity — or, to put it succinctly, action brings action.

Sitting around waiting for her is the wrong way to court Lady Luck. You must go out and find her. How? Well, humorist Stephen Leacock said, "I am a great believer in luck, and I find the harder I work, the more I have of it!"

I've tried to instill confidence, which is not to suggest that you become a braggart or a nonconformist. A great portion of one's personal attractiveness lies in his confidence, but don't go overboard. Remember, work toward a happy medium in most things. If you want to be different, fine; but don't act superior about it.

An important ingredient for success is the ability to make others like you. The chapter on personality will help toward that end. I've stressed it before, but it bears repetition: be kind to others and they

will be kind to you. I can't put it much better than Edgar Albert
Guest did:

> Let me be a little kinder
> Let me be a little blinder
> To the faults of those around me,
> Let me praise a little more.

Will You Have the Same Excuse Ten Years from Now?

I know there have been many gags about, "Do it now." Such as the
one about the employer who hung a sign counseling this in his
office, and the next day his accountant absconded with all the company funds, a clerk ran off with the employer's wife and a trusted
and essential employee went to work for a competitor. Well,
extremes aside, "Do it now" is a pretty good idea.

If you want to learn a new skill, start now! If you want to start
some sort of savings — bonds, funds or insurance — start now! I
know that the usual excuse for not starting now is "Oh, it will take
years for me to learn that" or "It will be years before that fund would
be worth any real money."

Well, here's a way to avoid that trap — just think of what your
excuse will be *ten years* from now! The same thing, probably! Don't
you see? A new skill may take five years to learn, but it will *still*
take five years to learn five years from today. Waiting will not make
the learning time any shorter, and waiting won't help your savings
any either.

Do it now, start now, or you will be quoting John Greenleaf Whit-
tier's:

> For of all sad words of tongue or pen,
> The saddest are these: "It might have been!"

Well, I'm sure that by now you must agree that your mind controls your life. Try the ideas in this book — use them — and you'll be
a happier person for it.

If I have taught you only that it is the training and organization
of the mind which alone can lead you toward a happy and successful
life, I have more than accomplished my purpose. I have to agree
with Shakespeare's, "There is nothing either good or bad, but
thinking makes it so."

The Intimate Enemy

by: **Guy Finley**

Reach New Heights in Your Journey to Higher Self-Awareness and Spiritual Growth

Life Changing Insights: "Freedom from what is unwanted by you begins with awakening to what is unseen *within* you."

True Encouragements: "Nothing can prevent the inwardly self-educating person from succeeding in life, because Wisdom *always* triumphs over adversity."

Self-Transforming Practices: "Meet each moment of your life with a wish *to understand* your inner condition, instead of looking for ways *to justify* it."

Higher Self-Command: "We must cease our struggles to be victorious over our perceived enemy and struggle instead to see through the layered illustration that *who we really are* has anything to lose."

Demy Size • Pages: 240
Price: Rs. 60/- • Postage: Rs. 10/-

The Meaning to KNOW THYSELF

by: **Dr. A.P. Sharma**

How to Attain Happiness and Good Life

Envy, jealousy, hatred, anger, fear, greed, selfishness, the negative feelings and emotions tend to poison our personalities and lead to tension and unhappiness.

The only way to check these feelings and enhance the positive aspects is through self-knowledge. One sure way to achieve inner harmony and happiness.

Now **"The Meaning to Know Thyself"** helps you attain it through the wisdom of the greatest and most revered minds and books. With the essence of Pluto, Aristotle, Buddha, Jiddu Krishnamurti and others all distilled and presented in most readable lucid style. Offering the most practical approach to decipher the unvirtuous thoughts, dispel anger, fear and selfishness and in turn achieve a pure self and attain inner harmony and happiness:

The Book Includes

✦ Buddhists' masters and monks lively discussions
✦ Comparative views of Eastern and Western philosophers
✦ Similes and myths from great masters.

Demy size, Pages: 128
Price: Rs. 60/- • Postage: Rs. 10/-

PEACE OF MIND
IN UNIQUE VERSES

by: **Hari Datt Sharma**

Achieve Peace of Mind
through Unique Verses

Money can buy many things but not peace of mind.
By buying this book you can attain peace of mind.
This whole book is written in simple verses,
as mind enjoys a strange bliss while reading verses

Peace of mind can only be attained through fighting the negative *emotions* like anger, jealousy, hatred, greed. Sound advice available from a variety of sources. But only those ideas get home well which are presented in an interesting and effective manner like above verses.

Now **Peace of Mind** brings you *lyrical poetry* on the attainment of peace that not only makes delightful and exciting reading, but also sticks in the mind. As you pace through its *elated verse* you'd discover who are the enemies of peace, what is inner peace, how to relax body and mind, why laughter is important, how sex can be constructive and destructive, why happiness is rare, how to let go worries, what's the law of compensation, how to make a happy home and a lot more. All presented in a never-before unputdownable lyrical package with sound ideas from Vedas, Upnishads and great philosophers of the world.

So no more philosophy or preaching—but sheer poetry of peace!

Demy size, Pages: 174
Price: Rs. 68/- • Postage: Rs. 10/-

Soul Healing

by: **Dr. Bruce Goldberg**

George overcame lung cancer and a life of smoking through hypnotic programming.

Mary tripled her immune system's response to AIDS with the help of age progression.

Now you, too, can learn to raise the vibrational rate of your soul (or subconscious mind) to stimulate your body's own natural healing processes. Explore several natural approaches to healing that include past life regression and future life progression, hypnotherapy, soulmates, angelic healing, near-death experiences, shamanic healing, acupuncture, meditation, yoga and the new physics.

The miracle of healing comes from within. After reading *Soul Healing,* you will never view your life and the universe in the same way again.

Demy Size • Pages: 288
Price: Rs. 75/- • Postage: Rs. 10/-

Banish Fears and Negativity
The Secret of Letting Go

By: **Guy Finley**

Whether you need to let go of a painful heartache, a destructive habit, a frightening worry or a nagging discontent, *Banish Fears and Negativity* shows you how to call on your own hidden powers and how they can take you through and beyond any challenge or problem. This book reveals the secret source of a brand-new kind of inner strength.

In the light of your new and higher self-understanding, emotional difficulties such as loneliness, fear, anxiety and frustration fade into nothingness as you happily discover they never really existed in the first place.

With a foreword by Desi Arnaz Jr., and introduction by Dr. Jesse Freeland, *Banish Fears and Negativity* is a pleasing balance of questions and answers, illustrative examples, truth tales, and stimulating dialogues that allow the reader to share in the exciting discoveries that lead up to lasting self-liberation.

This is a book for the discriminating, intelligent, and sensitive reader who is looking for *real* answers.

Demy Size • Pages: 240
Price: Rs. 60/- • Postage: Rs. 10/-

20 INSPIRATIONAL
KEYS FOR SUCCESS
IN YOUR JOB & CAREER

by: **Mike Murdock**

Many people in the world today feel as if their career is nothing more than work. They seem to have lost the joy in their livelihoods. Do you find yourself in this position? Are you asking yourself if it is possible to combine excellence on the job with enjoyment? Then the book you now hold can have one of the biggest impacts on your life — *if you read and apply what is contained inside!*

Sections include:

❑ 20 Keys for Working at Work.

❑ Questions to ask yourself about your job, your talents and your gifts.

❑ "Live With Balance" excerpt from *How To Be Happier in the Job You Sometimes Can't Stand* by Ross West.

❑ Inspiration and Motivation for the Workplace. Scriptures on work, your job, diligence in the easy-to-read *New International Version.*

❑ For the Entrepreneur or Business Owner.

❑ Inspiring and motivating quotes from noted professionals such as Zig Ziglar Kenneth Blanchard, J.C. Penny and Henry Ford.

❑ A Recommended Reading list that will help you maintain the cutting edge vital to success in the workplace.

Demy Size • Pages: 144
Price: Rs. 60/- • Postage: Rs. 10/-

HEALING THE PAST
FOR A VIBRANT FUTURE

by: **Arian Sarris**

Break free from the past

What prevents you from moving forward? You're stuck and you're scared. Something inside of you wants to escape. It's time to break free from your past. Find the courage to confront and slay the monsters (fears, insecurities, and self-destructive behaviors) which have held you back so long.

"Healing the Past" encourages you to face your past and overcome blocks that are in your way to personal growth. Don't worry, you won't have to do it alone — Author Arian Sarris teaches you how to contact your Higher Self, Guardian Angels, and a host of celestial beings ever ready to help! You can, yet, rescue your inner child and become the hero you were meant to be — not the victim.

Gain insights for fast and powerful changes, starting at the root of your evolution — Your soul. Sarris gives you plenty of nurturing and guidance to help you grow into your true self. Before you can begin the process of self transformation, you must reconstruct your past from this lifetime and many other lifetimes through profound yet simple change in your life-style.

- ✦ Set yourself on right track toward achieving highest goals
- ✦ Rid yourself of phobias, allergies, and self-complexes
- ✦ Heal past-life traumas to free centuries of trapped
- ✦ Energy

Demy size, Pages: 180
Price: Rs. 68/- • Postage: Rs. 10/-

Off-loading STRESS
At Work Place

by: **Paul Skye**

Relax your way to peak performance

With today's fast-paced life-style, being "stressed out" is usually the norm. From the mountains of papers on your desk and dealing with demanding managers, to trying to keep the office out of your personal life, you've experienced it—and it is taking its toll. Although most "experts" approach the subject from a psychological perspective, the reality is that stress is immediately reflected in the body, sapping your energy and well-being.

Now you can counteract the harmful effects of stress with simple exercises you can do most anywhere—even while you're at work! The exercises are based on traditional yoga practices, but they are state of the art in terms of their application. You don't need to be a contortionist or even be in great physical shape to benefit from these postures, breathing techniques, and meditations.

Just minutes a day is all it takes to improve your concentration, flush out toxins, balance your nervous system, and alleviate states of anger and anxiety. Plus, you'll get helpful tips on diet, time management, balancing home and work, and more. If *Thriving on chaos* sounds like the story of your life, it's time to take a deep breath, relax, and let this easy-to-use guide teach you the techniques you need to achieve your peak performance.

Demy size, Pages: 218
Price: Rs. 80/- • Postage: Rs. 10/-

CHAKRA WORKOUT
For Body, Mind & Spirit

*by: **Blawyn and Jones***

Are you dissatisfied with your
present level of physical and
spiritual energy? Are you
disillusioned by non-integrated
techniques that deal with either
your physical body or your
spiritual being, as if the two were
disassociated from each other? If the answer to either of those
questions is "yes", then this book can help.

With just a few minutes per day of dynamic movement and
consciously controlled breathing, you will begin to move your
Chi. or vital energy — and you will experience heightened levels
of physical energy, greater mental clarity, and a more fit and
flexible body. As your reservoir of energy increases, your joy
will increase, you will possess a greater capacity to function
happily and productively, and your spiritual progress will begin.

Chakra Workout gracefuly blends the traditions of *yoga*, sufism,
and taoism for the modern seeker. You will learn the ancient
techniques of rejuvenation from cultures around the world —
and achieve definitive results at your own pace, in the privacy
of your own home.

Meeting the demands of your daily obligations can drain you,
frustrate you ... and slowly kill you in both body and spirit.
Regain the vibrant physical and spiritual energy that is your
birthright — self-discovery begins here!

• Harness the healing energy inside your body
• Begin a path of spiritual transformation
• Discover the ultimate peace through meditation

Demy Size • Pages: 240• Price: Rs. 75/- • Postage: Rs. 8/-

The Portrait of a Complete Woman

by: **Dr. Avinash Chandra**, M.S.

This book is designed for a middle class or upper middle class woman who is well educated single or married, working or otherwise, but certainly interested to improve upon herself. For housewives, career women and models too.

It is certain to change your life style for a better happening. It can prove to be a marvellous instrument to discover a new woman in you. People expect you to play the perfect role model, a flawless performance. Perfect wife, perfect mother, perfect partner and perfect career woman also. With the heightened up expectation of the society are you ready for this super woman's role? Here is a chance for transformation, would you like to avail it?

Written by celebrity author of many best sellers Prof. (Dr.) Avinash Chandra, M.S., who is known for his innovative approach and down to the earth practical ideas • Nothing is more rewarding than discovering your own nature as a "Complete Woman" • Develop a pleasing and magnetic personality liked by all denounced by none • Learn the techniques to earn love, care, happiness, respect and attention • Encompass yourself towards the wide range of success.

Demy size, Pages: 304 • Price: Rs. 80/- • Postage: Rs. 10/-

Success Through POSITIVE THINKING

by: **S.P. Sharma**

Is half full better or half empty?

Choose right • Think better • Live well.

Present-day life has become too complex and complicated. There is a scramble for more and more. Money, power and wealth have become symbols of success and happiness. A confused sense of affairs and lopsided values that's leading to a lot of tension and distress.

Now "Success Through Positive Thinking" shows you the way out. Advocating a change of attitude through moderation, acceptance of things as they are, and inculcating of moral values. The result? A positive personality free of negative elements like anxiety, stress, greed, envy and jealousy!

An Overview
Success Through Positive Thinking shows you the right path to real happiness through:
+ A proper perspective on life
+ Meditations and prayer
+ Importance of work
+ Handling of criticism and slander
+ Knowing the difference between right and wrong, real and unreal
+ Proper channelizing of sexual and physical energy.

Demy size, Pages: 180
Price: Rs. 68/- • Postage: Rs. 10/-

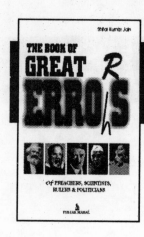

The Book of GREAT ERRORS
of Preaches, Scientists, Rulers & Politicians

by: **Shital Kumar Jain**

"To err is human" is an oft-repeated proverb.

It is used to cover up one's mistake as the author emphasizes. The book reveals how the mistakes of eminent persons holding positions of authority, as for example in Church, Government or Judiciary, exert profound influence on vast number of people in the society, nation and the world. The author tries to convey the message that such great errors may not get repeated for the betterment of future generations.

Know:

+ The grave mistakes committed by Heads of Religion and many Divinities.
+ The role of Semiotic Philosophy in environmental damage.
+ UK's neglect of Hitler's (mis)adventure.
+ Japan's attack on Pearl Harbour.
+ Mahatma Gandhi's rejection of Ambedkar's reform in Hinduism. And many more...............!

Demy size, Pages: 128
Price: Rs. 60/- • Postage: Rs. 10/-

Self-Defence against
Psychic Attacks
& Evil Spirits

by: **Dr. Bruce Goldberg**

What Invisible forces are attacking you?

Each day you are exposed to psychic attacks. They are responsible for a barrage of bad luck, physical ailments, accidents and even neuroses. Most physical attacks come in the form of noise pollution, threats of violence, negative people, and media advertisements. A small percentage are due to poltergeists or negative spirits.

Your only protection is your aura, the electromagnetic shield surrounding your physical body. If you keep this energy field strong, no psychic attack can harm you.

Now, *Self-Defence against Psychic Attacks & Evil Spirits* includes the newest research on energy fields, chakras, white magic, black magic, possession, and energy vampires. You will learn how to 'diagnose' and treat psychic attacks with a six-step plan for psychic self-defence. More than 55 exercises and scripts will help you promptly and effectively protect yourself and others. Dr. Goldberg explores the various types of psychic assaults through case histories from his Los Angeles hypnotherapy practice.

Demy size, Pages: 242
Price: Rs. 80/- • Postage: Rs. 10/-

Freedom from the
Self- punishing Thoughts

by: **Guy Finley**

Imagine how your life would flow *without* the weight of those weary inner voices constantly convincing you that "you can't", or complaining that someone else should be blamed for the way *you* feel. The weight of the world on your shoulders would be replaced by a bright, new sense of freedom. Fresh, new energies would flow. *You could choose to live the way YOU want.*

In *Freedom from the Self Punishing Thoughts*, Guy Finley reveals hundreds of Celestial, but down-to-earth, secrets of Self-Liberation that show you exactly how to be fully independent, and *free of any condition not to your liking*. Even the most difficult people won't be able to turn your head or test your temper. Enjoy solid, meaningful relationships founded *in conscious choice* — not *through self-defeating compromise*.

Learn the secrets of unlocking the door to your own Free Mind. Be empowered to break free of any self-punishing pattern, and make the discovery that who you really are is already everything you've ever wanted to be.

Demy Size • Pages: 192
Price: Rs. 60/- • Postage: Rs. 10/-
